Color of the River
A Journal of an American City
Cedar Rapids, Iowa

by

Steven D. Childs

authorHOUSE™

1663 LIBERTY DRIVE, SUITE 200
BLOOMINGTON, INDIANA 47403
(800) 839-8640
WWW.AUTHORHOUSE.COM

First published by AuthorHouse 06/16/05

ISBN: 1-4208-4296-X (sc)

Library of Congress Control Number: 2005903888

Printed in the United States of America
Bloomington, Indiana

This book is printed on acid-free paper.

ACKNOWLEDGEMENTS

I gleaned wonderful information from everyone listed below:

The Cedar Rapids Gazette Newspaper and Reid Magay
'Images of America,' Cedar Rapids, Iowa by George T. Henry and the History Center
'Glacial Age Floods' by E. Arthur Bettis, III and Deborah J. Quade and the Iowa
  Department of Natural Resources
Czech Village Assoc.
Linn County Historical Society (The History Center) Cedar Rapids, Iowa
Iowa State Historical Society, Iowa City
Islamic Cultural Center in Cedar Rapids, Imam Taha Tawil, Chairman
Cedar Rapids Historical Archives
Geobopological Survey at Worldwide Web
University of Iowa Museum of Natural History
'Glaciers Left Their Mark on the Mississippi River' by Ruth Nissen and Wisconsin Department
  Of Natural Resources
'Iowa's Archaeological Past,' by Lynn M. Alex, University of Iowa Press
Office of the State Archaeologist, University of Iowa
Arkansas Archaeological Survey
Staff at Makiki Community Library, Honolulu, Hawaii
'Insight Guides: Vietnam' by Hans Hofer and APA Productions

Mr. Ro Ngo of the Vietnamese Friendship Association of Cedar Rapids

African American Historical Museum and Cultural Center and Susan Kuecker, Curator

'Men of Ancient Iowa' by Marshall McKusick, Iowa State University Press

'A Brief Culture History of Iowa' by Shirley S. Schermer, William Green, and James M. Collins

Lloyd Gebhart, Denver, Colorado

'The Historic Period' by Carl A. Merry, University of Iowa

'State of Iowa History' by Dorothy Schwieder, Professor of History, Iowa State University

Iowa State History at SHG Resources

Iowa History at Yahoo Travel

Things To Do In Iowa/State History, Thingstodo.com

Gruwell Genealogy, Iowa, Royce Allen Gruwell

KWWL 7 News, Cedar Rapids, Iowa

Cedar Rapids Area Convention and Visitors Bureau

Cedar Rapids Area Connect/College and Universities Resources

City of Cedar Rapids Development Department/Demographics

History of Agriculture and Farm Machinery and Inventors, with Mary Bellis

Iowa.com

Fighting Hawkeyes in the Civil War prepared by Dwight D. Belles, Beloit, Kansas

Cedar Rapids Chamber of Commerce at www. CedarRapids.org/Chamber/History, ASP

RBA Hawaii Typing & Transcription Services, Kaneohe, HI

Lame Duck Graphics, Honolulu, HI
Mark Hunter, Cedar Rapids Historian
Special thanks to Richard and Judy Pohorsky, Cedar
Rapids, Iowa

**THIS BOOK IS DEDICATED TO MY
MOTHER,
LILLIAN KATHLEEN BURKE**

CONTENTS

<u>INTRODUCTION</u>

It is said that generally, we don't recognize actual history because we're all too busy living it. Day to day living for the average person hasn't fundamentally changed since the time of our ancestors, and events pass by that aren't important to us at the time. We are too busy protecting our children and making ends meet. Somebody must remember it, take the initiative, and write it down.

While seeking facts for this book, I've happily discovered that there are many individuals who have taken the time to do these exact things, and in doing so, they have compiled a wonderful and rich history of the progression of Cedar Rapids and its citizens.

These people made my job of compiling the events a bit easier.

It took a while to figure out what was to be written down, saved, shelved or not used at all. I didn't even know what sort of an outline to begin with or even know how to start one. Eventually, I figured it out and started writing. Now I will present the results to you in a chronological pattern.

I'm going to tell a story, a story that includes, among other things, the different ethnic people that comprise Cedar Rapids, Iowa, with whom I interacted with while growing up, including a little of their history. Furthermore, collective stories about life and growing up on the southwest side of this city during the late 1940's to the early 1960's. A personal portrait of sorts and how it all blends together.

There will be transitions in time throughout this book. First, going back to the Ice Age and how the area around Cedar Rapids was formed geologically. We will then go back to early Denizens, French and other explorers. We'll discover when and how Cedar Rapids was founded, its early people, traders, settlers and farmers that followed.

COLOR OF THE RIVER

CHAPTER ONE

CHAPTER ONE

I'm sitting here at a small desk in my apartment in Honolulu, Hawaii. The sun is dropping towards the horizon. Dark clouds hang over the Koolau mountains, heavy and unmoving. Late afternoon and it's sultry and warm, July 2002. For a reason, I still don't know, I decided to jot down a few words and thoughts on some paper. The blank backs of old menus from my now defunct catering business, and along with the pen from my checkbook, I start to scribble things down, words turning into sentences with no real syntax, incomprehensible scrawling. Yet, I continue writing stuff down; it's flowing out.

Most, if not all, Hawaiian homes and apartments have jalousie-type window slats, some made of wood, some of thick glass. These window slats overlap each other a bit and you crank them open to ventilate during the day and also during the night if needed on those hot summer evenings. Trade winds give steady breezes from the northeast so usually there's no need for air conditioners. Summer temperatures range from 90° days to 80° nights with light effortless currents of moving air passing through. During winter months the temperatures range between 80° highs to as low as the mid-sixties. You close the jalousie slats at night to keep the chill out along with a light blanket if needed. That's all you have to worry about here weather wise. It's the Tropic of Cancer. Blue skies and cloudy skies, champagne-colored beaches, blue azure and aqua green ocean, coconut and date palms at every turn, lush, growth-laden mountains with strange-shaped peaks; there's no need for furnaces here.

I'm writing more rapidly now, my mind is getting cluttered with too many images.

No furnaces needed, gee. I'm beginning to think back now, frantically transcribing, afraid of forgetting a thought before it's all written down, not wanting to lose anything. Useless dribble? Doesn't matter, just keep writing. I continue to describe events.

Cedar Rapids, when I was a kid. 1949, winter, coal furnace, snow, cold, our old house at 1602 K Street S.W..

Like most working class homes built during the early 1900's on the southwest side of Cedar Rapids, Iowa, ours had a coal-burning furnace to heat our house. Large, fat, asbestos-covered, octopus tentacles reaching upwards towards every room in the home. There was a coal storage room near the furnace. It could be filled through a wooden shoot on the side of the house directly into the coal storage bin that was a small room. About once a month, during wintertime, a truck from a coal company where the Czech and Slovak Museum and Library now sits, would come and back into the yard, between the houses. Then a man would hand shovel coal from the bed of a truck into the shoot, which rumbled down into the coal room. This operation was exciting enough to watch to actually let my mom pack and zip me into my one-piece, dark green snow suit and set me out on the porch steps to watch through frozen breath. "Do not move!" she would say, pointing a stern finger.

I would also sit on the basement steps sometimes to watch my older brother Larry scoop coal from the coal storage room directly into the open furnace door. Absolutely fascinating, I couldn't wait to be old enough to shovel that coal from the holding area into the furnace exactly like my brother. Stoking the fire with the long iron rod like some sort of steel worker, or better yet, a sailor deep in the bowels of a huge battleship, grown up sweaty manly stuff. "Want to give it a try?" Larry simply said one day. "Go ahead, try a shovel full," he mentioned. Okay, I was elated. However, I missed the open door of the furnace with a loud clang, spilling the entire load of coal everywhere except into the fiery cauldron I desperately wanted to feed. First try was a failure. When closed, the furnace door had a small little window you could peer through and see the glowing orange interior. The heat emanating first warmed your face then began to intensify until you had to pull away. I always waited until the very last second before my face would surely burst into flames. My brother calling me to hurry up the stairs before he shut the basement door. I didn't want to be caught down there in the cellar alone. It was kind of scary down there alone. Something might be hiding in that coal room. Time to go.

Dark gray smoke bellowed from our chimney during those winters in the late 1940's and early 1950's and left a light soot on the snow outside. I would press my finger against a frosted windowpane inside our warm house and look through the small hole I made. All the chimneys around the neighborhood with smoke puffing slowly away towards a slate-colored sky. All those coal furnaces doing their job. A nice, orderly warm world.

In later years when it finally became a chore to shovel coal during the winter, I decided to teach my younger brother Mike the joys of the art of coal transferring. Master to student. He tried one scoop, spilled it before reaching the opened furnace door, dropped the shovel and walked upstairs. No interest whatsoever. Unbelievable. I was stunned.

During the summer months, it was the Hubbard Ice guy, I don't recall too much, except the yellow wood-paneled truck with a heavy canvas flap covering the back end. The truck had red letters on each side that spelled "Ice". He would park on the street and walk with the block of ice on his leather-padded shoulder. The block was held between metal prongs and all balanced with his freehand. Mom's icebox was in the kitchen, of course. It had rusted light green paint with wooden doors. I would walk behind him watching the water drops hit the hot cement of the walkway leaving a dark spotted trail. Then follow him back out to the truck where he always gave me a chunk of ice to chew on.

"Okay now, stand back kid," as he got back into the truck and drove off leaving behind a small water fall of melted ice splashing onto the street. At the Jones County Fair in Monticello one year, my dad won a brand new robin's egg blue Plymouth on a $1 raffle ticket. He sold the car for a brand new refrigerator for mom. That was the end of the ice guy and the icebox was retired to the back porch.

I would suppose every family had its morning rituals back in those days.

"Did you empty the pee can yet?" my mom would ask us boys as we sat down for breakfast. During school days, it was always oatmeal and hot cocoa. The pee can was an empty one-pound Folgers coffee can we kept under the bed in our room. We were to use it instead of traipsing through our parents' bedroom, which was attached next to ours, or running into something while walking sleepily through a darkened house. This made sense to us. Mom usually complained to us about cleaning the toilet seat and linoleum floor from missed shots all the time. But over 50 years later, I think I just realized the real reason for the can. Anyway, this arrangement worked out pretty good until the protective ring around the top of one particular can came unattached and fell off after prolonged use, exposing a sharp edge along its circumference. Little brother swallowed a dime somehow one evening and decided if he went number two in the can the next morning, he would be able to retrieve the lost treasure. But, alas, while doing his job, lost his balance and sliced open a buttock. He was rushed out of the house to get stitched up. Myself, being the older brother and responsible somewhat for his immediate safety, was suspect with some kind of involvement. All I did was tell him what he had to do if he wanted the dime back. Mike has more adventures ahead and my failures at protecting him from harm.

My older brother Larry wasn't immune from this protecting a younger sibling thing either. He had to watch out for me. Here lies even more botched attempts at not only keeping himself out of trouble, but me not telling mom. My older brother was the coolest. Kind of like a version of James Dean. He wore brown loafers with white socks and denim jeans. The jeans were rolled up about four inches from the bottom, exposing the white socks. This ensemble was accompanied with either a white tee shirt or a dress shirt unbuttoned halfway down if he was styling. All his buddies looked the same. They were cool too. Circa 1952.

At this time, brother's main problem with mom was that he couldn't stay away from a place called Lindy's. Lindy's was a café-type restaurant, located at 232 ½ 16th Ave., S.W. near the Friendly Tavern located on the other side of J Street. For some reason, my mother didn't want us kids hanging around the place.

"Remember what I told you. Don't go around Lindy's, okay son?" she would warn.

"Okay mom, see you later," as he pushed through the new Rusco storm door and down the street into the night. The reason it was a new door is because previously, I had chased Mike across the living room with both arms outstretched in front of him to push open the front door and escape. His hands went right through the glass panes of the old door. More stitches.

I heard this exchange that night when Big Brother came home.

"Larry, is that you?"

"Yeah, mom."

"Are you hungry?"

"Nah."

"What'd you guys do tonight?"

"Not much."

"Been down to Lindy's?"

"Nah, just with the guys."

I knew what was coming next.

"Well, you're grounded and I don't want your friends around here either," she calmly ordered.

"Huh, jeez mom, how come?"

Mom didn't have to be a psychic to figure it out. He reeked of Lindy's. It emanated off of him like stinky feet. I could smell him from the bedroom. Lindy's had a unique scent, a combination of old, burnt hamburger grease and Cheetos corn curls. Very distinct. I was seven years old and knew where he'd been. It was like body odor, and he never figured it out.

Now Mike liked fire trucks. They fascinated him. His eyes would widen, and then get fixed whenever he heard sirens. His head slowly rotated back and forth like radar until he found the correct direction of the sound. Sometime during his discovery stage, he knew that if you pulled the red lever down on the box that was attached to the telephone pole at the end of our street, a fire truck would come. No one in the entire neighborhood had any idea what was going on, until about the third time the fire trucks came during that one summer. He would stand on his red wagon, reach up and pull the fire alarm. Then he would walk the wagon back home, sit down on the front porch and watch all the action. Mike knew how to have fun.

My folks came to Cedar Rapids from Council Bluffs, Iowa in 1941. Dad worked for the Milwaukee Road Railroad as a Night Yard Clerk and asked to be transferred to Cedar Rapids.

My father then changed jobs after a while and started delivering ice cream for Shomont Ice Cream Company, which was located at 104 1st Ave. N.W. near 1st Street. What a neat job for a kid's dad to have. He would drive the big truck up to K Street in front of our house for lunch once or twice a week. Every day the truck pulled up, dad would hand out Popsicles and fudgecicles to everyone. Needless to say, he was a big hit. He did this every time. I was famous. During the summer months, I sometimes got to ride on his route with him. He would drive around town delivering ice cream and then head out to the small communities surrounding Cedar Rapids and do the same. The ride along ended when Meadow Gold Dairies bought out Shomont.

Every once in a while when he worked for Meadow Gold, he'd still stop at home for a while and hand out ice cream bars and Popsicles to all of us kids. I was really proud of him. I'm sorry to say he was killed in an automobile accident near Dysart, Iowa while delivering his ice cream. It was 1961. I took the news hard.

We had the normal loving family. I was lucky in that aspect. I remember popcorn and Pepsi Cola in front of our television set we purchased in 1951. I also recall lying on the floor listening to 'Sky King' or adventures from the 'B Bar B' and other good radio programs every night. But, I immediately forgot all about the radio programs when the television arrived. Television was amazing. An actual play being performed before your very eyes. It was difficult to get the images on the screen perfect even when dad brought home a metal box, which was placed on top of the television set called a 'booster.' We watched most programs through a flickering snowy haze. It didn't matter. I never knew what the 'booster' was supposed to do. Little Brother always got confused between Captain Video and the Bishop Fulton Sheen program. To him they were the same person.

Christmas was a big deal, of course. One Christmas Eve, Mike and I were determined to finally figure this thing out. We lay at the end of the bed we shared and watched from our bedroom, through our parents' bedroom directly at the Christmas tree. We are going to see Santa do his thing. No more wondering.

Mom always put a glass of milk with the cookies she baked on a plate near the Christmas tree, and every year the milk glass was half empty and nothing but crumbs were left of the cookies when we awoke. Tonight would be the night we would actually witness this act. All we had to do is stay awake and watch Santa Claus perform his magic. You know what happened. Santa came, drank the milk, ate the cookies and left.

Didn't see anything, must have fallen asleep. Maybe next year.

There were a couple of huge lilac bushes in the back yard along with peonies my mom planted. It was interesting to watch the hundreds of ants crawling all over the buds before they opened up. I had a sand box way in the back near our garage. A couple of years before I started elementary school, I would play in the sandbox all day long with our dog 'Rusty' laying nearby. More large lilac bushes separated the sandbox from the alley. I would really get involved building miniature cities and roads using my toy trucks. I got so involved that sometimes I didn't want to stop and take time to go and use the bathroom. One time I decided to just stay out there, load my pants and continue solving the complex engineering problems as I continued building a town.

There was one small problem, when you're four years old, you just don't think ahead. I smelled bad. Rusty started looking at me strangely, but I ignored it and continued my roadwork. Finally, it all became too much to bear and it was getting late anyway. What to do now? I Couldn't yell out, "Hey, will somebody please change my poopy pants!" Before, when I was a baby, the stuff was automatically cleaned up and gone. I was stuck with this cargo. My mom finally yelled from the back porch, "Steeeeeve, time to come in." I must have had a funny look on my face because she paused then asked, "Are you okay?" Time to face the music. The next sequence of events is lost to me now. All I can remember is the switch from the willow tree whipping against my leg a couple of times. "Are you a baby? Huh, are you?" as she took me by the arm into the house. I liked that willow tree. It was shady and easy to climb, even though its thin branches were used more than once to discipline. I recalled the whole thing as "The Sand Box Incident."

Rusty, our Cocker Spaniel, was usually always with me at my side. He followed me everywhere. Once, I received a small turtle as a pet and kept it in a bowl with a little water and a rock to crawl onto. Rusty, at some point, placed his nose into the turtle's glass bowl, gingerly picked it up with his teeth, and went to the front door. Unknowingly, we let him out. He walked up to the end of the block with the turtle in his mouth, spit it out and came trotting back home. Rusty had become jealous because of all the attention I gave my new pet turtle. We thought the turtle had gotten loose someplace in the house, and we began a search. Rusty lay on a rug out of the way and watched with his eyes as we searched for the turtle. Mom realized what must have happened because Rusty never wanted out to go to the bathroom while I was still in the house. "Rusty...what did you do?" mom asked. Rusty gave up immediately. He got up and hid behind a chair. After a neighborhood search, sure enough, there the turtle was, exactly where Rusty dropped it in the grass at the edge of the sidewalk. It was unharmed. Rusty just wanted it out of the house.

I didn't play in the sandbox much after my dad chopped off the heads of two chickens on its wooden edge one afternoon. The severed head of the first chicken landed near my shoe and I watched its beak open and close a couple of times while its eyes slowly blinked. While my eyes were transfixed on the first one, the second chop startled me. I didn't get to see where the other chicken's head went because it jumped right out of my dad's hand, popped up and began chasing my dad around the back yard. It was actually running around for a couple of minutes without its head. My dad was laughing at his own antics but had a worried look on his face as the headless chicken, with wings flopping around and blood spurting everywhere continued chasing him.

This graphic scene is ingrained in my brain. Yeah, that did it. No more outback alone in my sandbox with Rusty.

My brother Larry had a couple of female classmates that lived within a block or two of our house. One day, I remember in particular, when no one was home and Larry was supposed to be babysitting me, he had three or four of his friends over that day hanging out along with one of the girls. At one point, he just seemed to disappear. He actually had the audacity to sneak in the house and lock everyone else out. This included everyone except the neighborhood girl. At that time, I had no idea what was going on. It seemed to be some sort of hide and seek game they were all playing, but for some reason, this situation seemed to be very upsetting for my brother's buddies. I didn't mind at all, because I got to hang out with the older guys who were, by now, running and stumbling around the outside of the house. Either banging on the doors or performing a sort of bizarre dance, which consisted of popping up and down like unrhythmic jack in the boxes, arms flaying, trying to peek into the two bedroom windows facing 16th Avenue. What kind of game was this? Look at these guys. I noticed their macabre dance became intensified around one particular window.

"Stevie, hey Stevie, come here. Find out what your brother's doing!" one of the guys said. With that, he picked me up and lifted me high into the air and pressed my face against the window. Right at that moment, as my nose touched the glass pane, a yellowish watermarked shade instantly snapped down from inside. I saw nothing. "Whadya see, whadya see!" they clamored, gathering around. Noticing I was now capitulated into the man of the moment, I said, "I saw my brother and a girl." Pressing closer, one asked in a hushed voice, "What were they doing?" I stayed silent. "Huh, come on…come on!" he stammered. I looked around at their seriousness. "Tell us!" they pleaded, wringing their hands and trying to look back into the still shaded window. "I dunno, he pulled the shade down before I could see." Their faces went blank. Eyes staring unbelievably. It's not what they wanted to hear. I immediately became useless again. Half-hearted attempts to breach the house floundered and they slowly drifted away, resigned in the fact they were to be witnesses to nothing. I waited on the front porch. The girl eventually emerged and walked home. Big brother, soon after. My memory and perhaps discretion doesn't let me recall much more after that.

I have no idea when the house siding salesman showed up at our house. It must have been around 1950. He talked to my dad about new siding for the house. Dad went for it, and I remember this conversation verbatim. "Mr. Childs, this siding will last you 50 years." It was an almost lime green with little white sprinkles and put on rather quickly. I drove by the old place in 2002, over 50 years later. The green siding is still there…still intact. I must say, it still looks like it did in 1950. A solid product, didn't chip, fall off, fade or anything, just as the salesman said. This has certainly changed.

On the opposite side of the coal furnace in the basement was a washing area with a hand water pump. It was red in color and had a waterspout that the water ran from. It reminded me of a large tongue. Mom had a ringer-type washer. After you washed the clothes, you would wring the clothing individually into a basket, then hung dried the still wet shirts and pants outside on the clothesline. A myriad of endless ironing followed.

In the basement there was also a cupboard area with shelves that held canned fruits and vegetables. All I remember were the canned peaches and tomatoes. It was covered in the front with a piece of cloth on a rod that slid open when you needed one of those Mason jars full of something. I hid in that same pantry once when my mom was at St. Luke's having my brother Mike. Grandma Baker, my mom's mom, came from Council Bluffs to watch over the house during that period. She was a bit too stern for my spoiled young taste, and I also didn't quite understand where my mom was. So I just stepped inside the curtain and waited. I hid down there all day from her. Poor old Grandma was frantic over my whereabouts and becoming a little hysterical. I still didn't move. My secret departure was working. This will teach her I mused. Later in the afternoon, my Brother came home and joined the search, but to no avail. However, when a neighbor mentioned calling the police, I decided I'd better show up somewhere.

I nonchalantly parted the cloth, climbed the basement stairs to the kitchen and walked outside and sat down on the back porch steps. I don't remember any spanking or discipline I received or what happened after that episode except a cuff on the back of my head from my brother. "What's the matter with you?" he quipped.

The basement has another story. My dad went duck hunting one weekend with some friends. He shot some ducks and brought them home in the trunk of the car. They had been placed in an old potato sack. Dad took the sack downstairs to the basement to sit before he cleaned and dressed them. Later, after an hour or two, he went downstairs to finally start defeathering and cleaning the ducks. He squatted down and untied the top of the potato sack, holding his quarry. Apparently, one of the ducks had been only stunned. He revived and came flying out quacking with his wings fluttering. Dad fell back in surprise and I bounced off at least two walls trying to get back up the stairs. Feathers were in the air as the wounded fowl flew around the confines of our basement looking for a way out. A wild duck loose and on a rampage with dad, Larry and I chasing after it. Around and around we went—the furnace and coal room, the pantry, the washing machine area, everywhere. We just couldn't corner it. The duck hid out in the basement for a couple of days. Mom refused to do laundry or anything down there while the duck was loose, which created a problem. Someone finally cornered it and a day later, the poor duck was our supper. Dad seemed to have trouble with ducks and chickens.

Mike and I had a babysitter watch us now and then. She was a neighborhood girl who went to school with Larry and lived down the block. For a couple of kids like Mike and I, she was the greatest thing ever. All she did was make sure none of us killed each other or got killed. Other than that, everything was pretty much wide open. We enjoyed seeing her show up. She had a younger sister that was really cute. I thought she could have been a movie star. So, of course, there were boys following them around everywhere. Mike and I never put two and two together. Do you remember the dime Mike swallowed? It came from some guys looking around for our babysitter and her sister one evening. We gave them directions to their house and we were rewarded with a dime each. One of the boys' exact words were, "Go and buy some ice cream or something," after handing us the dimes.

The babysitter would tell us, "Run, run, get into bed and pretend you're asleep, hurry!" when she would see our parents' headlights pull up outside. Giggling, we would pull the covers over us just in time. Loved that girl. Stayed up as long as we wanted.

One summer after Grandma passed away, Grandpa Baker stayed with us. Mom made up a place for him in a large walk-in closet just off our bedroom. The closet had a stairway with a door that led up into the attic. The attic was another scary place when you're young. It didn't help when one day Larry and a cousin of ours hid up there. It was bad enough that I had to go and get something. As I opened the door to ascend the stairs, I heard something. I raised my head towards the top of the stairs and saw two large ghostly figures just standing there peering down at me. Both of the ghost figures started making "Booooing" sounds and stomped down the stairs toward me. Stunned and in fear, I went careening off the doorway out into the living room screaming for help. With my mom in hand, I cautiously peeked around the corner through my parents' bedroom into mine. There sat both my brother and my cousin on the edge of the bed holding white sheets and laughing hysterically. It seemed funny to both of them, but I was mad and complained bitterly to my mom with no avail.

When Grandpa had breakfast with us, he used to pour molasses over his oatmeal. He put molasses on everything. For some reason, this upset me. "Sugar, Grandpa...you're suppose to put sugar on you oatmeal," I would say as I watched him stir it all together. Grandpa Baker always wore work pants with a flannel shirt and a brown cardigan- type sweater buttoned most of the way up. This was both his winter and summer attire.

We had two pine trees in front of the house on either side that looked like Christmas trees. Grandpa decided to trim the lower branches for us. The pine branches came down to the ground, but after the trim job, the bottom branches were at least five feet from the ground, clean and neat, I thought. Dad came home from work, stood there for a while looking at them and walked into the house—never said anything. I'm sure he must have mentioned something to mom in private like, "What the hell happened to the trees?" I don't know why, but those evergreen branches never even tried to grow back and still looked exactly like the day my grandfather cut them after 50 years. The trees were finally removed completely a while back. Grandpa Baker also put together a ladder from scrap wood he found in the garage. Our family used that old ladder for years, even after we moved to 1927 L Street, S.W.

It was around these times when our family had two more arrivals in the house. Another brother, Mark, born in 1953 and a sister, Sherri, born a year later in 1954. I was eight or nine years old by then, so they were pretty much out of the picture as far as causing trouble for anyone. Big Brother Larry and my tag-along nemesis, Mike, were my only world at that time. When I graduated from high school in 1963, Mark and Sherri were still in grade school. I don't have an abundance of stories about them as I do with Larry and Mike while growing up. I just don't remember either of my younger siblings ever having to be run to the hospital once or twice every summer to have a gaping wound sewn up. Mark and Sherri both stayed mostly out of trouble, I guess. I didn't see or hear anything. They probably did their, 'Let's give mom gray hair' stuff after the rest of us had already left home. We lost Sherri in an accident in 1973 when she was 19. I remember an incredible moving road show Mark and I took traveling on a tour of dementia throughout the southland one winter and spring in the late 1970's. A wild four-month automobile trip that would fill enough pages for some sort of strange Hunter S. Thompson Book. I'd have to use a pseudonym. It was great fun and a good adventure.

Our neighborhood on the southwest side was pretty much Czech. Older wood-framed homes painted white, some having the gingerbread-type trim along the large open front porches.

I went to elementary school at Van Buren. It was over on 14th avenue SW and 'L' Street and built in 1884. When my friends and I walked home from school, we either hit one of my friends Bubi's house for goodies or the corner store. They were in opposite directions, but both were on the way home. In the early grades of elementary school, I often wondered why my grandparents were called Grandma and Grandpa, and most everyone else's were called Bubi (Babi) and Jeda (Djeda). The old couple that sat out on their porch swing across the street from our house were called Bubi and Jeda. I thought that's what their names actually were. Next door to them a playmate of mine couldn't wait until his Bubi and Jeda were coming over again to visit. Six or seven years old, it didn't make sense. It seemed everybody had a Bubi and Jeda except me.

The fellow over at the corner store at 15th Ave. and L Street S.W. put up with a lot from rowdy, over-exuberant children.

I remember one day when we were trying to say swear words in Czech. He interrupted us a minute and said, "You silly children. You are not saying it right

"Now listen to me..." he would say. Then slowly pronounce the bad words to us. We would then repeat them back to him. We would always ask him what the Czech words meant.

"Never mind," he would always say, returning back behind the counter. He was a kind old gentleman just trying to help us with our foreign language lessons. His store was one of the stops on my dad's ice cream route.

The guy from a National Yoyo distributor would show up every spring and dazzle us kids after school with all the Yoyo tricks in his repertoire. It was a regular show. He was an Asian, which made the whole thing even more fascinating and exotic. Everyone would either buy a Yoyo immediately afterwards or run home and ask for money to buy one. The small grocery store had a large assortment of penny candy, so scores of school children met there before and after school. Van Buren Elementary had a gravel playground with all the normal playground equipment of the time. Three tether ball poles (which became May poles every May 1st.), a jungle gym and a row of monkey bars of different heights. These were always good for looking at the girls' underwear, then tease, "I see London, I see France, I see..." well, you know. I have never seen an elementary school with a gravel playground. We never thought anything about it. Skinned elbows and knees were normal throughout the school year. During the spring thaw or rainstorm, streams of water would drain off the streets and also the alley that crossed behind the school and separated the playground from residential homes. At recess we would dam these small rivulets up, causing a huge artificial lake to form. The custodian would have them all destroyed by next recess and we would have to rebuild all over again. Busy little engineers we were. Gravel was our main ingredient. Another elementary school full of kids of Czech Heritage was Hayes on 19th Avenue and Hayes Street and D Street S.W. Students at Van Buren didn't know much about Hayes or its students during those times except that they had grass for a playground.

Both elementary schools came together to form the 1957 class of Wilson Junior High. It was a natural meld. Interstate 380 came through the Van Buren school district in the 1970's and the solid old school was demolished. Its stone dedication plate is now located at the Linn County History Center along with the stone plates from Jackson, Tyler and Polk, other old outdated grade schools. I asked a friend of mine living in Cedar Rapids to go down and check out the stone dedication plate that had been removed and saved from the aged schools. In doing so, he uncovered and solved a fifty-year mystery for both of us. It seems that one particular name in question on the stone marker for Van Buren was that of a certain architect. Upon close examination, he found out someone between the years of 1884 and 1955, had carved directly into the stone and changed the 'L' in this person's name into a 'C'; you cannot imagine how hilarious this name became to a bunch of 10 or 11-year olds when we noticed the gentleman's name while playing one recess and not knowing it had been altered years earlier. "The name's a fake!" my friend proclaimed to me over the telephone. "The real name is Fulkerson!" Cold case file solved.

According to a 1983 Gazette article written by Reid Magay about the history of Cedar Rapids immigrants, Czechs from the old country filtered down to the Iowa River area and the rest of Johnson County south of Cedar Rapids from Southwestern Wisconsin by Ox Teams. Where these folks originated from before that,

I don't know. Families then slowly began migrating up to the southern part of Cedar Rapids along the Cedar River. This last trek took place in the 1850's. These early people were mostly farmers and found out they could buy inexpensive land nearer to Cedar Rapids. Other of these folks came for political or religious reasons. A better life, nothing else. That's the name of the game for any immigrant. By the 1860's most had filtered into Cedar Rapids southeast side of town.

After the Civil War, friends and relatives started showing up and by the late 1870's became about 12% of the population here as skilled craftsmen, businessmen and laborers. What probably sustained these people were the fraternal organizations they organized, such as the Cesko-Slovanska Podporujici Spolko (CSPS) known today as the Czechoslovak Society of America. This was founded in 1879. Furthermore, the Western Fraternal Life Association, originally known as the ZCBJ. I remember that being near downtown on Third Street and 12th Avenue S.E. The Czechs apparently took care of their own pretty good. There also was an athletic group called the Sokols, known for their gymnastics. All the groups are still functioning to this day, something solid for the early people to hang onto along with their great grandchildren and regular citizens of Cedar Rapids.

Then, of course, Bohemi town. Oh, yeah! It was Las Vegas to a 10- or 11-year-old kid on the southwest side, the Forbidden City. At that time, there were only two places off limits for us. The river and Bohemi town.

"Hey mom, is it okay if we walk down to Bohemi Town?"

"No! You don't need to go down there." (Probably because there seemed to be a tavern or two on every street.)

"Oh, okay." But it was straight down to Kosek's 5 and 10 or Sykora's for a kolace. Ted's Pharmacy was good for a cherry coke at the soda fountain, but seemed to adult for us. We went and strolled around everywhere. If you could put a dollar together, you were in. Three kids could put a buck together. It might take a week but you could do it. The Me Too, Sixteenth Avenue Market and the Shell gas station. The whole place is called Czech Village now. You should have been there back then. I'm happy someone had good sense to preserve it all. It was, and still is, such an integral part of the southwest side.

There used to be a fire station down on 'C' Street between 12th and 13th Avenues. The city moved the firemen into a new firehouse and left a perfectly good building right there at Riverside Park. It didn't take long for an entrepreneur to step up. One day at Wilson Junior High, a gentleman showed up at our student council meeting. He explained to us what he intended to do with the 'Old Firehouse.' I was a member of the Wilson Student Council at the time. "Ladies and Gentlemen, I am so excited to announce to you that I am going to turn the old fire station at Riverside Park into a new recreation center for teenagers." He went on, "We'll have dancing and entertainment every Friday and Saturday nights." Fridays would be only for the junior high students and Saturday for high school.

Alright, this sounds pretty good so far, then, in a very secretive low voice he dropped the hammer to the group of 12- to 14-year-olds.

"Our first personality to perform will be Jimmy Clanton." He went on to say that he would appear at our initial grand opening on such and such a date if he could find the time. "But pleeeeze don't mention this to anybody, because we want it to be a secret surprise, and that we'll have loads of fun." The girls in attendance took the bait—hook, line, and sinker. They told *'everybody'*. Keeping a 13-year-old girl from telling a secret is impossible. Basic psychology is in play here. On the given date, the place was packed with young people, myself included. Of course, Jimmy Clanton never showed up and the amazing thing was, it didn't matter. The place was a big hit, regardless. My friends and I spent many a weekend there socializing, dancing and generally hanging out. Entertainment besides dancing were groups like the 'Jefferson Jesters,' a group of high school students who mimed a parody of hit songs of that era. They were good. To us it was adult entertainment. The Riverside Recreation Center along with the Y.M.C.A. Teen Canteen on the corner of 1st Avenue and 5th Street in the Y.M.C.A. building were a good deal for us kids during the adolescent stage of our lives.

As I look back, I'm glad somebody had enough sense to give us something to do. Cedar Rapids, Iowa. We had everything and didn't even know it. It is ugly in the winter, there's no doubt. Gray, old, beat up, cold with dreary blackened snow, but back then we didn't notice. When you're a kid, it was nothing but good times.

The Penick and Ford plant owned the Cedar Rapids skyline along with Quaker Oats early on, each on opposite sides of the river. A fellow named George Douglas and his father George Douglas, Sr. first started out with a company called Northstar, a cereal mill, the perfect place at the perfect time. Different grains were grown all over the area. Later, it officially became the world famous Quaker Oats. The Douglas boys left the cereal company and started Douglas & Company for the manufacturer of cornstarch. After a horrible explosion and fire in 1919, which killed scores of workers and destroyed the plant, was rebuilt. After a while, it emerged as Penick and Ford. It made starch, corn syrup, molasses and many other corn-based products.

Penick and Company employed a lot of Cedar Rapidians at the time. It was right next to Riverside Park. An adult or someone older would usually accompany myself and a friend or two over to the Park to play. Riverside is located on the riverside of 'C' Street S.W. It is one of the city's oldest parks along with Bever and Ellis. It was established in 1894. We used to play along the stream that ran through the park and eventually emptied directly into the Cedar River. We also entertained ourselves in the small wading pool that was available to cool off in. A nice pavilion in the middle of the park added the perfect touch. It was ideal for a kid living in the neighborhood. The cedar flooded one year clear up to the roof of that pavilion. All that stuff is gone now. In fact, most of Riverside

Park is also gone. It's one quarter of the size it used to be. Even the Riverside Recreation Center, I remember so well.

I don't know which product caused the aroma that covered the west side, but because of Penick and Ford, Riverside Park had a distinct and pungent odor, a sort of sour, stink that permeated the entire area along with half the city. Quaker Oats manufacturing process wasn't as bad as Penicks, but also noticeable when you sniffed the air. Quakers was a nicer cooked cereal sort of smell. You lived with it and got used to it. The smell seemed normal. If it wasn't there, you wondered if everything was okay, so was Cedar Rapids then.

THE ICE AGE AND PALEO INDIANS

I'm not a geologist or an archaeologist, so what follows was taken from many different sources named in the acknowledgment section of this book. I then mixed and blended the knowledge, some of the words I copied verbatim.

Before the prairies and before the corn, there was ice. Ice sheets at one time or another covered most of Iowa during the Pleistocene age, which lasted from around two million up to 10,000 years ago.

The Mississippi River (we'll call it the Mississippi River for now) like all normal rivers, was in a constant state of flux during this stage of time, changing courses all the time. Various different forms of the river flowed through our area for more than a million of those two million years. It's hard to understand the constant changes taking place throughout this time period—the fluctuation caused by the warming, then freezing up again of ice sheets during the Pleistocene era.

The ice age in Iowa receded, then built up again over and over during this vast expanse of time. The upper Mississippi Valley, as we know it, was primarily shaped during the most recent glacial stage of the Great Ice Age, known as the Wisconsin Period. The glacier during the Wisconsin Period covered most of where Cedar Rapids is currently located. (See Diagram 1)

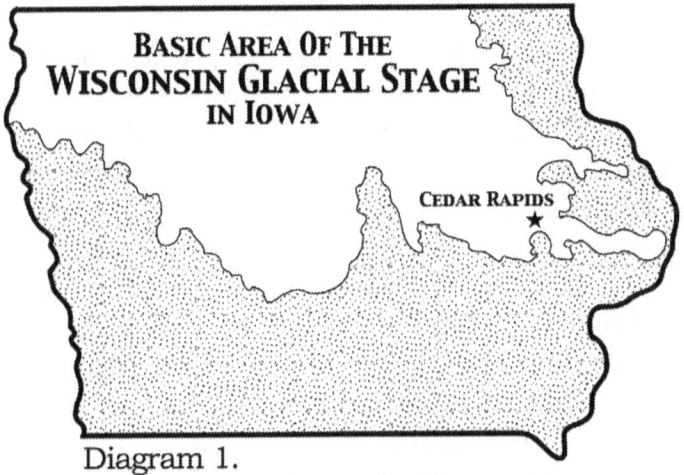

Diagram 1.

Area of Wisconsin Glacial Stage that covered
Cedar Rapids and Iowa.

(redrawn and simplified from
Men Of Ancient Iowa
by Marshall M℃Kusick)

The recent Wisconsin Glacial Period started from around 90,000 to 75,000 years ago and stopped 12,000 years ago when the North American climate began to warm again. This is likely when the Early Paleo Indians began to drift into and enter the area around Cedar Rapids. However, the landscape at that time would not be recognizable today.

On the fringes of this massive undulating ice sheet, the Minnesota, Wisconsin and Iowa regions were populated by large animals called Mega fauna, which thrived in the cold climate on the margins of the receding glacier. These giant-sized animals included mastodons, mammoths, and caribou, and before that, there were giant beavers, sloths, musk ox, and even camels. Since the orientation of the Mississippi was north to south, many of the ancient fishes just moved south as northern waters of the river grew to cold. The fish reversed up back north as the glacial sheets retreated. That's why the ancient fish are still around and live in the waters of the Upper Mississippi River. The gar, sturgeon and paddlefish, for instance, gravitated and survived.

The big story is the melting of those enormous ice sheets that at their maximum was as much as 10,000 feet deep and covered hundreds of square miles. When it warmed up, the ice released tremendous amounts of water forming huge glacial lakes. The largest of these glacial lakes covered parts of Minnesota, North Dakota and the Canadian Provinces of Manitoba, Saskatchewan and Ontario. The southern discharge outlet from this massive lake was called Glacial River Warren, the early mother of the Mississippi. Another glacial lake, which covered the Lake Superior basin, was called Lake Duluth. It's outlet river was called the St. Croix River and it drained into the River Warren. In Wisconsin another glacial lake drained itself first into one river and then another, which also emptied into the River Warren. During the thousands of years that River Warren carried water south from all the glacier lakes, the Mississippi River Valley was carved side to side and the resulting valley was approximately 250 feet deeper than it is today. There is evidence that this last valley wasn't the first time this cycle or series of events took place carving out river valleys draining from the melting ice mass, just the more recent or last time. Therefore, between 20,000 and 9,500 years ago, the Mississippi River Valley served as a conduit for the sometime sudden drainage of the large glacial lakes. The tremendous flow of water southward was finally diminished and the Mississippi River became the only and most important large stream in the area. The valley formed so quickly, long branching tributary river systems formed after the Mississippi was formed. Through the ages, however, tributaries were finally cut and drained into the main channel of the Mississippi Valley. This is where the Iowa and Cedar River enter the picture, along with hundreds of others and by 10,000 B.C. Iowa was ice-free.

After the ice age, environmental studies at the Iowa State University show that the ice age coniferous forest (evergreens, pine and spruces) was replaced by deciduous forest (trees that shed their leaves or fruits) about 8500 B.C. By 6500 B.C. these forests were composed largely of oak and then replaced by prairie grasses.

The Wisconsin glacial stage reached its maximum stage around 40,000 years ago. So much ice was locked up in the Continental ice sheet, it lowered the world's sea level by over 400 feet. The Bering Strait, which is 56 miles wide and separates Siberia from Alaska nowadays. But, back then a 700 to 1300 mile wide land bridge furnished an easy route of travel for fauna and finally, man. There was also an important small sliver of land in Western Alaska, along the coast, that remained ice-free. It was a direct road into North America...and eventually onto Iowa.

Known Iowa archaeology begins about 10,000 B.C. Twelve thousand years ago, humankind, the first Native Americans, entered the territory we know as Iowa, equipped to cope with cold, ice age conditions, following closely behind the retreating glaciers. These early occupants of the region lived in small and highly mobile bands and were primarily hunters of the mammoth and other large mammals of the Iowan Tundra. Their tools included lance-shaped spear points and specialized butchering tools. As the climate changed and warmed, Iowa's first inhabitants developed a more diversified living style as they learned to exploit a more varied environment. Most known sites of this period represent kill sites or butchering areas. Paleo Indian sites are very difficult to find, partly because of low population density. The best Paleo Indian site in Iowa is in Cedar County where an entire cache of Clovis Arrow Points was accidentally recovered from a plowed field. These Paleo sites are far and in between.

Archaeologists define four prehistoric eras in the Mississippi Valley. First the <u>Paleo-Indian Era</u>, which

I just described, second the <u>Archaic Era</u>, which is the longest, beginning about 8,000 B.C. to around 2,500 years ago. This age represents Native American adaptation to the waning of the ice age and the development of more effective means for using an increasingly wide range of natural resources available after the large mammal extinctions. This supported continuous population growth, which meant sedentary living instead of wondering around with the entire extended family all the time. A variety of local plants were domesticated and grown with the expansion of prairie and then deciduous forest, which added to the gathering of food supplies. They hunted bison, deer, elk, and smaller animals. Tool types included grooved axes, nutting stones (mortar), manos, (pestle) metates, (grinding stone) and others. These tools were used in pounding, grinding, crushing and chopping activities in plant processing. The third, the <u>Woodland Era</u> from 2,500 to about 1,000 years ago represents the growth of communities with economies based on a mix of hunting, gathering, and agriculture. The climate and landforms had stabilized to resemble those of today. A dense population and a more complex social organization also characterized the Woodland Era. Furthermore, a lot more experimentation with agriculture went on.

These early people had leadership and cultural distinctions along with technological innovations including fired clay pottery and bow and arrow. Bow hunting is shown by the small arrow points found which replaced the larger spear points. This era is approximately when Mound Building began. <u>The Mississippi Era</u> was the fourth and last of the prehistoric eras. It began 900 to 1,000 years ago. These folks depended more heavily on agriculture. There were multi-village communities numbering in the thousands. These communities also built ceremonial temple mounds.

According to the office of the State Archaeologist, the first earthen burial mounds may have appeared in Iowa as early as 1,000 B.C. and are associated with the Red Ocher Complex. Red Ocher Mounds are found across a broad area of both eastern and Midwestern North America. People interned their dead in sub-floor pits or within the mound fill itself most commonly as bundle burials. Red Ocher, a powdered form of Hematite, was applied all over and surrounding the remains. Grave goods, fashioned from exotic raw materials such as copper, galena, (crystal) slate and flint. Included were polished stone, gorgets, (marine shell jewelry). Leaf-shaped bifaces (two-sided stone tools) and straight stemmed projectile points. The distant origins illustrate the broad connections the Midwestern people had. Grave goods from Woodland Mississippi Era mounds include fine, thin, highly decorated pottery, copper axes and pins, carved sheets of Mica, Galena cubes, (crystal) fresh water and marine shell beads with containers, finely chipped Obsideian, Chaledony, (quartz) and Chert (flint) projectile points. These materials came from the Atlantic Coast, the Rocky Mountains, the Great Lakes and the Gulf of Mexico. You can see by these artifacts that there was commerce between people over the entire continent.

Piling up earth one basket load at a time, Indians raised mounds to heights of up to 13 feet. Mounds not only were used for burials of important authority figures, but also to have symbols for their origin stories or some kind of renewal ceremonies.

Many mound groups and villages occur along the Mississippi River and its tributaries, and most famous are the Effigy Mounds shaped like birds, bears, lizards and occasionally human remains are found in Iowa and adjacent states. In Iowa, mounds are concentrated along the Mississippi River Bluffs north of Dubuque and along the lower reaches of the Turkey, Yellow and Upper Iowa Rivers. Mounds also occur throughout east central Iowa along the middle reaches of the Iowa, Cedar and Wapsipinicon Rivers. The prehistoric Indians were living and building mounds where we live today. (See Diagram 2.)

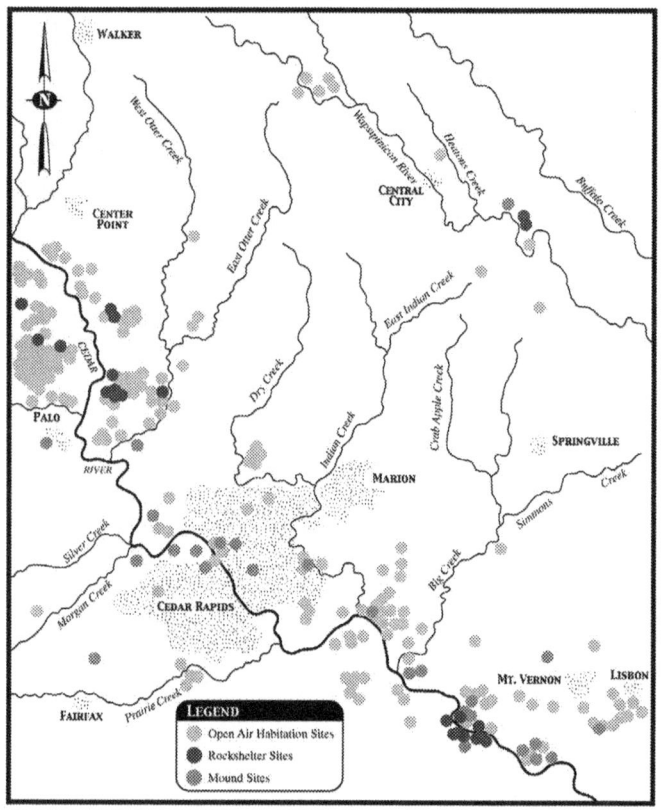

PREHISTORIC ARCHAEOLOGICAL SITES IN THE CEDAR RAPIDS AREA
(Courtesy Of The History Center)

Diagram 2.

The Woodland Era and Mississippi Era people who constructed these mounds may have lived in dispersed groups, occupying sites such as rock shelters during the winter and merging with related families at River Valley locations during the milder seasons. These families apparently constructed the effigy mounds over a period of time, perhaps in an attempt to maintain harmony between themselves and the natural world. They may also have served as territorial markers.

It's difficult to connect ancient mounds with specific historic Indian peoples in Iowa. Some later groups, including the ancestors of the Ioway and Otoe, occasionally buried their dead in the old mound fills and some may have constructed new mounds, but the tradition of mound building was apparently all forgotten by the time their descendants occupied the state.

Today, fewer than 1,500 mound sites survive in Iowa. They are recognized and respected as ancient Native American cemeteries and are protected by State law.

Now, getting back to explaining the Mississippi Era, the Native American economies at that time were supported by craft specialization and the production of corn, beans and squash. In Eastern Iowa, the Oneota culture was prevalent. The Oneota culture was probably directly ancestral to the Ioway Indians encountered by the first European explorers when they entered Iowa.

Late prehistoric or late Mississippi Era includes the years leading up to 1,650 A.D. These times marked the beginning of a distinctive adaptation to the tall prairie grasses and short grass plains. Improved corn varieties, garden surpluses, new storage methods, earth lodge houses and a total complex social organization were common. Bison meat was a common item in the diet, and hides were processed for clothing, robes, and coverings for teepees and lodges. Bison bones were modified into a variety of tools such as scapula hoes used in gardening and digging. Villages were situated on low terraces above the flood plains of rivers, streams, and lakeshores. The entire population throughout the fall, winter, and spring may have occupied large permanent villages. Smaller, temporary campsites were used for seasonal procurement of resources. During the summer, a communal Bison hunt or the establishment of small campsites for gardening purposes may have led to the temporary leaving of large homesteads by most of the residents.

Several Oneota sites in northeastern and also northwestern Iowa bridge the prehistoric and historic eras, 1640 to 1700 A.D. Early French trade goods such as glass beads, finger rings and gunflints which were found at sites dominated by Native American-made materials. In Iowa, the term protohistoric denotes a period when European articles were showing up before European people started to make extensive written records of the area.

Indian groups residing in or using portions of Iowa seasonally in protohistoric times included the Ioway, Otoe, Omaha, Missouri and the Dakota. These groups were essentially stationary, but elements of their population made wide ranging seasonal forays for hunting and warfare. After around 1650, European competition for tribal alliances and trade, along with European diseases, drastically changed the relationships among these Indian groups. Tribal populations declined and who owned what territories became scrambled and undetermined. In Iowa, the tribes mentioned above (Ioway, Otoe, Omaha, Missouri and Dakota) gave way to Great Lakes groups including the Sauk, Mesquakie (Fox) Winnebago and Potawatomi. So, it was, so it became. History falls forward into Chapter 2.

COLOR OF THE RIVER

CHAPTER TWO

CHAPTER TWO

Mom used to send me to the Y.M.C.A. over on 1ˢᵗ Avenue N.E. on Saturday morning. A friend and I would catch the bus by ourselves and ride downtown. We used to pretend the bus was a submarine and we were operating it. When the bus turned, we would yell, "Turn, turn...crash dive, crash dive!" and when it would straighten out, we would talk into our hands, "Okay...okay, come up to periscope depth." All the way downtown. We'd have swim class at the 'Y' first, then play ping pong in the game room, or something else like board games, until it was movie time. Everyone would retire to the movie room, sit orderly cross-legged on the floor and eat our sack lunches everyone had brought. My main fare was always Velveeta cheese with sliced dill pickles. I loved those sandwiches—every Saturday, Velveeta with dill pickles.

"Wouldn't you like a peanut butter and jelly this time?" mom would ask. "Nope." After lunch they would start setting up the projector and screen. Anticipation was high. A large 15 or 20-inch film reel would be attached to the projector. The screen was enclosed in a tube attached to a tripod. They would straighten the tube out from the tripod and then pull the white, silvery screen down from the tube apparatus, and snap it into place at the bottom. Showtime! The projector whirled to life, and the lights went off. 5-4-3-2-1…numbers that sequentially reversed themselves appeared on the screen. The movie began, and Tom Mix, Gene Autrey or Roy Rogers would materialize, and the shoot-em-up black and white action movie went on from there. Great stuff! Everyone blinked their eyes at each other when the lights finally came on at the end. Whew! Back to reality. My goodness…where was I? The Y.M.C.A. also had a summer camp somewhere on the Wapsipinican River. Camp 'Wapsie Y.' We bunked in cabins with five or six other children you didn't really know. The counselor for that particular cabin stayed in a private room in the back. Every morning after a head count, he would check to see if your bed was properly made up. He did this with much ceremony as he bounced a quarter on the top of your neatly made bed. By golly, it had better bounce up from the tight cover or he completely tore the bedding up and directed you to redo it. This continued until everyone's bed was perfect. Then, and only then could you proceed to breakfast. We would go on nature hikes with our counselors showing and explaining certain flora. Canoeing was a favorite thing to do for myself. We ate in a large log cabin-type dining hall with everything already prepared. We always had free time during our week's stay to explore and hang out with new-made friends.

The boy scout camp, Waubeek at Waubeek, Iowa also on the Wapsipinicon was a bit different and stricter than camp Wapsie—more military in nature. You lived in tents with wooden floors. On the bright side, you always got to bunk with your best buddy. Everything also had to be neat and clean, especially how your clothing and personal items were stored. The nature hikes in the past were now more like troop movements. The scoutmasters carried binoculars and sheaved hunting knives during our hikes. I came up through the ranks, so to speak. Webelo Cub Scout in Pack 26, at Van Buren to boy scout. I even collected a few 'merit badges' along the way—to my credit, in the boy scouts. The counselors at 'Wapsie Y' were high school kids. The scoutmasters at Waubeek were a lot older.

These guys seemed a lot more serious about what was going on, with constant head counts. We did all the normal camp stuff, hiking and canoeing. One year, we organized a mock raid across the river to the girl scout camp. About 10 canoes participated and when someone on the other side spotted us coming, a general alarm went up, and the girls ran around screaming hysterically anticipating our arrival like we were some sort of invading Viking marauders with rape and pillage on our minds. Their excited responses and fright scared us and left us wondering what to do next. As I think back, what were those young girls really anticipating? Definitely not a bunch of fruitcake twelve-year-olds who could barely keep a canoe on course, let alone paddle it correctly. Anyway, it was all in fun and we never made it to shore, but I'm sure there was a phone call or two from the girl scout director of their camp to our camp afterwards. I must say, even to a 12-year-old, it was rather exciting to see the girls running around in a complete panic and shock at our swift war-like approach. A raid of conquerors called off mostly because we didn't have a clue what to do next. On the last weekend, they trooped us all along a darkened trail at night into the woods. The leader or point guy walked with a flashlight shining out from in front of him. Then he halted at a certain point and turned solemnly towards us. He then spoke these words, "Beyond this point there will be no talking. We are about to enter the zone of silence." All right, no more words can be spoken. We then tripped and stumbled forward like good soldiers going to our death. When we arrived, above us we saw a large group of other camp Waubeek campers sitting around a half circle, like in a Roman amphitheatre or coliseum. Down in the center was a bon fire. We filtered in and sat down in our reserved area. Our leaders disappeared. It was definitely an 'Indian' type atmosphere. You felt it—don't screw up the sanctity of this place, you thought, because this is real. No one spoke a word or messed around which was difficult for a young kid. They had us hooked. What a strange new experience. It was almost religious like, and then a man walked out from the side into the front of the campfire. He was dressed like an Indian and had a fox skin with the fox head attached that sat on top of his head. The rest of the fox's pelt was draped, with all its sheen, hanging down behind him. This was the real deal. He then began to announce the evening's festivities. Codes of honor were recited, mini plays were performed and speeches were given.

The last act of the evening involved two scouts, one who sat in front of the other. The kid in the back had a sheet or blanket over him so that all you saw was the guy in the front. The guy in the back had his arms positioned and stretched around the man in front. The man in the front had his arms at his sides, yet it was invisible to the people in the audience. In the performance the man in front was to eat from a plate of food set on a table before him. Though his arms and hands were hidden and not functional, the man in back used his arms, as he pretended to be the arms and hands of the man in front. He picked up the food from the plate and the search for his mouth began. What a mess it was, as the antics of the man in back pretending to be the hands of the man in front and not being able to see anything, trying to pick up and place the food in the mouth of the man in front. It was one of the funniest performances I ever saw. No one knew what was going to happen next and it was hilarious.

Camp Waubek and scouting was definitely fun for me. My mother still has all of our cub scout and boy scout shirts. She proudly showed them to Mike and I during our recent visit home.

My brother Mike had a couple of bad summers in a row. At one point, a city work crew was replacing the sewer line along the Linwood Cemetery side of 'L' Street. They dug a deep trench and placed the concrete replacement sewer pipe cylinders alongside ready to roll in. Back then the city used smudge pots to line the trench at night warning pedestrians and drivers to be careful of the excavation in that area of construction.

Smudge pots from that time were round, ball like metal containers filled with kerosene. These things had some kind of wick that ignited and would literally burn all night. These smudge pots were eventually replaced with the technology of blinking yellow lights. We used to 'borrow' the pots and use them in our wood fort above the creek that ran through Linwood Cemetery. After continued use of starting and extinguishing the pots over and over, we ran out of fuel. We needed to have them refueled. What to do? "Hey Mikey, take these down to our garage and fill them with the gasoline used for the lawnmower." Mike was elated. His young face filled with pride as I handed him the two empty containers. The pots had small chains attached to them enabling them to be held in place with a metal spike at the construction site. 'An important mission to help my big brother,' he must have thought. What an honor. 'Maybe I'll even be accepted by these guys, so they won't try to run away from me all the time.' Off he went dragging the two smudge pots behind him on the chains like unruly pets, looking back now and then to see how they were coming along, happy to be helpful. After 30 minutes, I began wondering what happened to Mike. I swear, just at that exact time, I heard the sound of fire trucks. I walked away from our fort towards home. I then noticed black smoke rising up over our neighborhood. Walking more briskly now, I started to get a sick feeling. A couple of my friends ran past me and then turned their heads back towards me with horrified looks. "It's your house! Your house is on fire!" Well, it wasn't the house, it was the garage—the interior, to be exact. Last fall, my two neighborhood friends and I decided to start a paper drive and sell the old newspapers to a recycler to earn spending money. We had tons of newsprint and magazines stacked to the rafters along one entire wall, all neatly tied together. The firemen made quick work of the fire and our garage was saved. My newspaper drive was finished—all burned up. My brother Mike was all right, but he had small burns on his forehead, hands and nose. His eyebrows were gone. It didn't occur to any of us that kerosene burned and gasoline exploded. To us, they were the same thing. Mike dutifully filled the smudge pots with gasoline from the one-gallon can for the lawn mower as he was told. For some unexplainable reason, he decided to see if it would work. He lighted a match and whooom! Everything ignited in a flash. How close was that? I dread to think if we would have tried to light the pots in the confines of our underground fort.

A couple of weeks later, our gang was warding off some rivals over in Linwood Cemetery. We had to retreat back to 'L' Street and the still uncovered ditch. There were too many of them and they were very aggressive—with rocks and dirt clods flying. We held them to a standstill. It seemed that they had had enough and figured they drove us far enough back, but they had only retired across an open lot to the edge of the small creek where they hunkered down. There were three or four of us sitting in a row down in the sewer line ditch along with Mike. He turned out to be a good soldier, but too young to really help. There was some scuffling above us and dirt filtered down the side of the open ditch onto our backs. All of a sudden I looked up and saw a blonde girl with a large brick held over her head. Down came the brick right on top of Mike's head. Blood splattered everywhere, and I was stunned. For a moment, I just stared at my dazed and bewildered brother. The girl ran back to her area and disappeared. I was outraged! I took Mike home for the umpteenth time bleeding—then off to the hospital. My friend and I retrieved our BB guns, mine a Daisy—and we both went on a hunt. We were unable to catch up with anyone since they had disappeared. We combed most of the cemetery and outlying neighborhood to no avail. We didn't see any of them. We later discovered who the girl was and where she lived. We also found out that she had two mean older brothers, so she was spared for the meantime.

Our next summer was more of the same—I held Mike's hand and walked him home with his head bleeding again. "Mom, pleeeease..." I pleaded. "I can't watch him every minute." Two weeks prior to that incident, Mike tripped and fell onto a burnt out trash pile along an alley as he was running behind us and hurt his hand. He skidded on his hands to break a fall and gashed it on some broken glass within the charred pile. (Back then it was lawful to burn leaves and trash.) Mike was like a loose cannon or an out-of-control locomotive. I'm not kidding, it was constant mayhem. I was a nervous wreck and at one point, one of my buddies suggested we just tie him up and leave him somewhere. That made sense, "Don't forget to take your brother with you today…and please watch him this time," mom would shout after me as I tried to sneak out alone. "Mommmmmmm," I begged. "Take your brother!" she would yell after me. God help me. "Okay, come on, I'm going up the hill." ('L' Street) Well, what can I say? We tied him up to a chair inside an abandoned house that was ready to be refurbished. It didn't seem right, but I needed a break.

After messing around for twenty or thirty minutes, I couldn't take it any longer and went back and released my poor young brother from his bonds. I threatened him with his life if he told mom, then added, "And she won't let you play with us guys anymore." To this day, Mike has stayed silent.

One afternoon, I was playing in the living room when one of Mike's friends came flying down from our upstairs bedroom and ran wild-eyed out the back door without muttering a word. A couple of minutes later, Mike nonchalantly said, "Mom, I think there's a fire upstairs." Well yeah…half the upstairs bedroom was aflame, and everyone adjourned out to 20th Avenue in the street. I remember there were firemen on the roof of our house chopping a large hole with axes. The entire neighborhood was watching and I became a bit embarrassed. However, the fire was put out and once again, the Cedar Rapids Fire Department saved the day. They were really quick to respond and saved our home. Of course, the entire upstairs was gutted and had to be refinished although its structure was sound. At least we didn't have to move. Mike's story was that nobody knew what had happened. The insurance company and fire department decided it was a bare light bulb that was pressed against the insulation in storage areas along one wall of the long bedroom that took up the upstairs. There was cupboard like doors that opened up to this area, and you could crawl inside and pretend like it was a fort or something. Thirty years later, Mike confessed. "Mom, remember that fire we had?" It seems he and his friend were 'camping out' in the upstairs storage area and decided to build a campfire. End of story.

The following years, for some reason, were spent at either our grandparents' farm near Council Bluffs, an uncle's farm nearby, another aunt and uncle's farm outside of Sioux City and at a town called Ruthven, Iowa near Spencer and Arnold's Park with cousins. All of these places were absolutely wonderful. The farms and small towns were endless with stuff to do. My first roller coaster ride was at Arnold's Park on Spirit Lake. These were full-blown working farms with boundless rows of corn, hogs, chickens and cattle. Large barns full of hay…I loved the smell of the farm—earthy stuff. The first few days on the farm, Mike and I ran around acting crazy, stepping with bare feet into freshly made "cow pies," licking the salt lick constantly and jumping into the cattle's water tank to splash around. We would make condominiums out of the hay bales in the loft and chase chickens. Plus, introductions to some strange cousins whose ideas of fun made my friends and I back home look like preschoolers. I loved those summer days down on the farm.

If you were 10 or 11 years old back in the 1950's, Linwood Cemetery was the greatest playground to ever play in. It was a virtual paradise that bordered 6th Street on the west, parts of 16th Avenue on the north, 'L'

Street on the east and Wilson Avenue on the south. It encompassed a huge expanse that was heavily wooded on its edges with gravesite and large areas of open fields. A small creek ran through the wooded eastern side. Eighteenth Avenue was the northern limit for a couple of blocks and ran up to 'L' Street. Above this area in the cemetery itself, there was a small service road where old flowers, ferns, wreaths and whatever was thrown over the side with a 30-degree angle down to the bottom. All along this road we would have winter sled runs.

The individual sled runs had names like, 'The Nutcracker' and 'Dead Man's Curve.' Every year they were located in the same places. There were four or five other good slides known for their dangerous sledding right down into people's back yards bordering 18th Avenue. Flying down the runs, dodging trees during the thrilling ride in the snow and the cold was exhilarating. It seemed that every kid in the neighborhood was up there with sleds and rosy cheeks. It was a winter social event. "Did you do Dead man's yet?" some kid would ask. "Yeah, twice already," you'd lie. We used to pull our sleds up into the cemetery from the 'L' Street side, skim down the slopes, and then drag the sled back up again over and over all day long.

Summer in the cemetery was the best, we started out exploring the place, graduated to playing army, and built forts. During our playtimes at the cemetery, there was a time one spring when a group of teenaged girls would trail home from Wilson High School. Wilson was a high school before Jefferson was built. When the girls would walk home in groups, most of them would head towards their homes. The girls that lived on the other side of 6th Street S.W. would cut through Linwood and stop at a certain place on a bend in the lane among the gravestones. There on the side of the road, they would light up and smoke a forbidden cigarette. We noticed them the first time while playing army, and we stopped to observe what they were doing. They were pretending to be older than their 16 or 17 years. Giving discerning smiles to us showed that they were more mature than we were, they knew their tight skirts and sweaters were a magnet for young boys. They flirted, teased, smiled and primped. We just stood there in silence staring—our eyes glued to them. They would then get up, brush themselves off and slowly continue to walk home, glancing back once or twice to see if we were still watching.

We saw the same girls at times bring with them new friends for a few times that spring. We would stumble over each other trying to get to the bend in the road before they arrived. We would wait for them with stupid, silly grins, then they were no more, gone one day—never to return. We soon returned to our army games. The vision and memory of those girls will ever be ingrained in my mind.

The 'L' Street guys, as far as we were concerned, owned Linwood. It was our property, oh yes, usurpers would try to gain control of our area, but we would usually run them out with threats that often turned into dirt clod, rock, and spear fights. Once in a while the older guys would 'hang out' up there and there was nothing we could do except wait them out until they lost interest. We protected our domain; however, there was no reason for getting beaten up. We loved Linwood Cemetery—it had everything a young boy could ever want.

In later years, a school mate approached me about earning some bounty money by capturing prairie dogs. We would catch prairie dogs and turn them into the cemetery caretaker, as he had a 20-cent bounty for each capture. We were so proficient that the money just rolled in. We would catch so many that we had to bring along a burlap bag to keep them in. After a couple of days, the caretaker informed us, "Just bring me the two front paws boys, okay?" No problem, we brought with us our boy scout hatchets for the hunt. Not a bad summer-time job, except for the chopping off of the front paws portion. Yep, my friend had a sure plan and it was really nice. He said, "Listen, this is how we do it. Do you have an old fishing pole?" "Yeah, I think so," I said. Then he said, "Bring it with you tomorrow, no need to bring a hook or sinker."

When I met up with him the following day, he also had a fishing pole. In a hushed voice, he said, "First you sneak up on the hole and quietly place a noose around its circumference with your line. Then you reel off about 20 feet and sit down." "Okay," I whispered. He said, "Now start whistling something." "Okay," I said, and like magic, a little prairie dog's head would pop up and look around from the hole. Then, "Wham!" my buddy snagged his first one around the neck with a jerk and then reeled in the stumbling, rolling prairie dog. In the burlap bag it went—slam, bang, all afternoon. "Ka ching!" After the second day when we handed the caretaker a gunny sack chuck full of half-strangled animals is when he decided it would be a lot better if we only brought him the front paws. It became a bit messy, but we didn't think anything about it. I'm sure some animal rights activist would be cringing right now. We literally cleaned out the entire population. As I look back, I think we were cheated.

The woods, open spaces, and a meandering creek made up Linwood Cemetery back then. A lot of undeveloped areas to play in. We built a solid timber fort in the woods above the creek. You couldn't see it until you walked right up on it, and then another wooden plank clubhouse type fort on the edge of the meadow on the opposite side of the creek. It was visible to anyone passing by.

The large hill that overlooked 'L' Street acted as our main fort area. It had a 360° view. A square hole in the ground was dug out about 4 ft. by 4 ft. It had a log roof that was covered with cardboard then dirt. You could almost stand up inside. We made a fireplace and had a small wood table down there. The entrance had two steps with a trap door to close behind you. We would all huddle around the table for hours in our hideout. Endless games of Army/Hide and Seek, dividing up into teams and running into the thick weeds and woods—then arguing over who was shot and who wasn't, as we lay in ambush along the heavily vegetated creek like marines in the South Pacific.

Sometimes damming up the water and splashing around in the large muddy pool we made contributed to how we spent most of our summer vacations up there. What a wonderful place to get lost in. We would do bad things to preserve our territory. We would destroy other kids' forts that had the audacity to stake claim, threaten the younger ones with torture if they came around. We weren't afraid to use the ultimate weapon if needed, but only if needed...the BB gun. This went on summer after summer until one day, like clock work, we became interested in girls. It's like it happened to all of us at once during the school year in Junior High. You couldn't be hanging around trying to impress the girls and play kids' army games at the same time. We somehow knew you couldn't do both.

We began doing more grown men things like trying to dam up Prairie Creek (which we found to be impossible) or jumping from the train trestle into the creek moments before a freight train rolled across. Ice hockey with sticks and a rock, bon fires in the winter, ice-skating and chipping holes in the ice to ice fish at Prairie Creek that became our new habitat. We soon forgot about Linwood Cemetery and gave up all our forts. Prairie Creek was also heavily wooded, but for some reason or another, we never built a fort there. We would explore the entire area from where it emptied into the Cedar River, clear back up behind Hawkeye Downs.

Our favorite place was back at the railroad trestle by Jones Park. I was 13 years old when I got spanked by my dad on orders from my mom. It was, of course, because of Prairie Creek.

"I told him not to go down to that creek!" mom would say angrily when dad got home from work. After a couple of swipes with the belt, mom would intervene, "Okay, okay, that's enough."

During the last disciplining procedure, the phone rang and everything stopped while mom went to answer it. Thankfully, the phone call was for me. I answered and it was my girlfriend on the other end of the line. My first real girl friend, you could say, asked me, "Hi, I just thought I'd call and see what you were doing?" What could I say? Geez, my dad was in the process of whipping my behind with his belt for playing like a kid in a muddy creek. Definitely not adult stuff. I replied, "Oh nothing, just watching the television." My legs were stinging.

The last belt dance, well, I got to watch my little brother Mike do that dance number a couple of times. He couldn't stay away from Prairie Creek either. Little by little, Prairie Creek drifted from my mind and by high school, it too was forgotten like Linwood Cemetery.

My older brother Larry sent all his siblings t-shirts from Biloxi, Mississippi for Christmas while he was in the Air Force. Emblazoned on the front of the t-shirt was a Kessler Air Force Base insignia. Larry was training at Kessler Air Force Base. I wore that t-shirt everywhere—school, to play. When Larry came home on leave, he taught me the proper military way to change altitudes for an aircraft. He told me that he could and would break any code I devised within one hour. He also showed me how he wore his wristwatch. It was slipped to the side of his wrist and not on the top of it like normal. He said all the personnel wore their watches exactly like that so they could record the time quick when working. They didn't have to turn their arm for the correct time when intercepting foreign codes.

All of these things were amazing to me, and I wanted to know more. Larry was ready to oblige, he broke my code in about 10 minutes. I wasn't very bright; it was in letter form and I used a different symbol for every letter in the alphabet. He showed me my mistake and how he did it so quickly. "See these…" he said, "These are the letter 'E,' and these here are probably 'A's, as his finger roamed over the symbols. "The two most common letters in the English language." He continued on, "So you can see, it wouldn't take someone very long to put it all together." My eyes just opened to something new, different and interesting.

Larry, dad and I were standing out in the front yard one day when he was on leave, when friends of mine had called from across the street. It was time to go and play army. My father and brother leaned close to me and in a knowingly tranquil voice said, "Don't chase them too far.

Tell the guys on your side to go ahead after them and make noise. You and another guy can hold up and hide out." I listened intently. "Sooner or later, the people you're chasing will double back and cross your path. That's when you stand up and let them have it." It didn't work that day; however, eventually it did work. Larry left for Germany soon after that time.

I can't remember exactly when, but we started including, in our activities, a young, black kid from school. Most of the guys I hung out with had a sense of humor, or I guess at that age it's called silliness. The new guy would go along with most anything any of us would come up with. He not only had the right attributes, he came with a good background. His older

61

sister went through the same school system as our brothers did. So it was never a shock to any of our parents that a black kid showed up with us one day. His family lived a couple of blocks from Penick and Ford. Riverside Park and the river itself were within striking distance when we were hanging out around his house. "Don't play near the river, honey," his mother would warn him. "Yeah, okay," and straight to the river we went.

One Saturday, I was having lunch at his home when I first noticed how beautiful his mom was. She had a warm, pleasant smile on her face all the time as she moved about the kitchen and setting down some bowls in front of her son and I. She said, "You boys hungry today…do you like tomato soup Steve?" "Yeah, my mom makes it too." With that, she filled our bowls from a sauce pan. "This is a little different from my mom's!" I told my friend that was sitting next to me. He shrugged his shoulders, uninterested. We began slurping it down with bread and butter. "What do you mean, sweetheart?" his mom said from the kitchen counter. "It's just soup." "I dunno, my mom's is thicker or something." I said, as I was spooning it in. "I think my mom uses milk," I added. "Well, we use water here." "Oh," I said sheepishly. I was a kid but still knew I had probably just hurt her in some way and was immediately ashamed of it. Stupid, stupid person, I thought to myself. I'm invited into my friend's home for a quick lunch and then insult their hospitality. I didn't mean to, and there was nothing I could do to make it up. I had to get that off of my chest after all these years.

One afternoon, we were down inside of our fort on the hill at Linwood with our new buddy. It was his first time in our hideout, and he was impressed. His eyes roamed over all our neat stuff, with a huge grin on his face. "Yeah, we got these smudge pots from the street down there," someone said. "Does the fireplace really work?" he asked. "Oh yeah," I said, as I retrieved a box of stick matches I took from our kitchen. The fireplace was a hole dug into the side of the dirt wall with a piece of rusty thin sheet metal we shaped into a cylinder for the smoke stack. It stuck out a couple of inches above the ground. We used up most of our supplies of firewood and paper that afternoon to make sure the new kid knew we were cool and knew how to build forts. One fall day, while walking home from school, three of us decided to pull a prank and pretended to beat each other up. We wanted to see what passing motorists would do. First, my friends pretended beating on me, then our black friend and I began beating on our buddy. No one responded, but when we began beating on our black friend, all hell broke loose. Passing cars honked at us, people hanging out their windows and yelling at us. Then all of a sudden an elderly woman came out onto her porch and scolded us. She threatened to call the police. "You, leave him alone, you bad boys!" she screamed. Off we ran, a little embarrassed. It was fun hanging around with someone different. It introduced us to something never experienced before. At one point, after checking out our forts in Linwood, my black friend wanted us to scout some areas along the river by Penick and Ford to build another fort, near the area he lived in. It was a great idea since no one can ever have enough forts. As we were walking along the river bank he stopped and said, "You guys want to see something really neat?" We followed him farther on down the river bank over boulders and through thickets and that's when he showed us one of the wildest things we ever discovered or knew existed. An entire world of exploration lay before us—a storm sewer outlet, opening out to the river that was quite large. The opening was concrete and eight feet from top to bottom. The following day, we were packed for bear hunting with flashlights, matches and peanut butter sandwiches. Remembering the 1950's movie, "Them," where giant ants lived in the sewer systems of Los Angeles, we bravely entered the sewer outlet. I remember the exhilaration of investigating and searching for something unknown. The stream of cold water was about six inches deep and flowed out spilling into the Cedar River. We slowly entered, advancing into complete darkness with our Converse tennis shoes, sloshing slowly forward. After 10 minutes of walking, we encountered our first dilemma. There was another large opening coming in from the side, not as big as the main cavern we were in, but sizeable. 'Should we enter this one...? No, let's continue on.' Oh, man, we were deep in here now—onward, splashing along, flashlights scanning the top and sides as we pressed ahead. We paused, noticing another side opening. "It looks smaller up ahead," we whispered to each other. "Let's just go a little further," someone said. The cylindrical tube we were in was smaller for us now and we had to watch our heads as we proceeded on. Then suddenly there was a light up ahead. "Look, a ladder going up," one of the guys mentioned and climbed up the rebar-type ladder extending out from the cement. "It's a manhole cover opening," he called down to us. We had hit a street sewer opening somewhere . As we came upon more of them, we became much braver and bolstered with more knowledge. We then decided we would stop exploring after we climbed the last street sewer. We had been wandering around the Cedar Rapids sewer system for three hours and had climbed the ladder, pushed aside the heavy manhole cover to discover that we were in the middle of Hayes Elementary School's playground. We emerged with blinking eyes as we dusted ourselves off and babbled excitedly to each other on our way home. We invited a few tourist to join us on our journeys beneath the earth for a couple of days after, pretending to be sewer guide's extraordinaire.

My friend and his family were the only African Americans living in our neighborhood. I never did notice any other black families living in the area or when we would hang around his front yard. There may have been many black families living and working in our neighborhood, but I was too young to take notice of anything. When I was at Wilson Junior High, our eighth grade wrestling team went on our first road trip to McKinley Junior High and it was along the way there that I observed black people walking along sidewalks, coming and going at various stores and businesses or driving cars on the streets. There were black people waiting at the bus stops, unloading trucks, children playing in their front yards, moms sitting on their porches. All of a sudden I thought, "Oh, oh, wait a minute. What's going on, are we still in Cedar Rapids?"

My eyes were glued to the outside of the window of the school bus as I watched the activities in stunned silence. With feigned bravado, we disembarked the school bus and entered McKinley's main boys' dressing room. Our team shuffled silently like robots, white knuckles clutching our gym bags as we passed through rows of lockers into our own smaller visitor's dressing room. The southwest side was nothing like this—my first taste of culture shock.

In 1820, something called the *Missouri Compromise* made the Iowa Territory a non-slave area. Prior to the Civil War there were few people with African heritage living in Cedar Rapids. A woman by the name of Ellen Taylor, who in 1864 may have been the first African American. In 1865, the number was verified at 10, and the city's total population at that time was estimated at around 3,900 after the war. A wave of African Americans immigrated northward into Cedar Rapids—not because of any underground railroad in place, hiding and moving slaves before or during the Civil War here, but because of family or friends that had already arrived and lived here. Writing letters or sending messages to prospective people to move here was a common thing. This was true for those who wanted a better life. By 1880, there were approximately 200 or so former slaves and native residents living here. These people survived by doing manual labor jobs and domestic-type work. Bethel African Methodist Episcopal Church in Cedar Rapids was started by these same people. It was the first African American church in the area. By 1908, the black population was between 300 to 400 souls. A mass movement of people to Cedar Rapids from the south occurred in 1910, and by 1918 approximately 1,000 African Americans lived here. Everything meshed together for the following 50 years. By 1960, 1,500 families became an inherent part of the city. During the mid-60's, some aspects of the African American population in Cedar Rapids became more aware of their rights as individuals and what it meant to them. It seemed to me that during my high school years the west side folks were mellower than those living on the east side probably because I was just involved with my own little plane of existence on the west side. What I do remember is that no one burned anything down in Cedar Rapids during the protest and riots in the mid-sixties that plagued other cities.

I was 12 years old when we entered our first year at Wilson Junior High School. The Van Buren and Hayes Elementary Schools came together to become the new seventh grade. There were cute girls that attended Van Buren; however, by the time sixth grade rolled around, they had become more like troublesome sisters. From kindergarten, the boys had to deal with them, always telling the playground monitor on every infraction of the rules. They couldn't wait to tattle tail and tell anyone who would listen. The girls had some sort of stupid mothering complex, which was embarrassing at times. How could anyone see them in any other light except a bothersome nuisance? After six years of this, along came the Hayes girls. They were like a breath of fresh air, as far as us guys were concerned. To add to this, everyone's hormones were beginning to stir at once. Playing Army over at Linwood was dropping off drastically, even our own Van Buren girls began looking and acting differently. The psychology of adolescence took over like stampeding elephants trampling everything. We were following behind the girls in the halls, stopping and running into each other at their quick glances back, while they were giggling at us. Not knowing what to do next, they were like magnets. Yes, seventh grade was a year of bewilderment.

After things settled down for a while in the eighth grade, we found ourselves doing things together with the girls, especially during the winter months of the school year. Hay rack rides at Upmeyers Stables, ice skating at Manhattan-Robbins, Prairie Creek, the pond at Jones Park, and the best place ever for social winter interaction was the flooded and frozen Hayes Field. Hayes Field had a "warming house" with a heater. I have no idea if it was electric, propane, oil, or what, but I do know it cranked out some heat and it was hot. I loved that warming house—sitting across from each other, all scrunched in together, legs pressed together from knees to hips. I can still smell the wet wool mittens that accidentally came in contact with the heater. The confines of the small, warm room fostered a myriad of shy smiles and sensations if you were lucky enough to be sitting next to a girl. All this was usually met with either disdain or profound innocence. Who would know the difference? It was usually a former Hayes girl who won at Pom-Pom Pull Away—tagging the boys effortlessly as they tried to avoid her.

Baby blue angora sweaters and earmuffs, hockey skates, racers and figure skates with teeth on the leading edges, bright red cheeks with wisps of breath, sweaty foreheads and invigoration—it makes one feel sorry for the kids who never experienced winter.

One block down on 20th Avenue was a large white house with a brick chimney protruding 3 or 4 feet upwards from the peak of the roof. About once every summer, an old man living with his wife would carry out a long, narrow painter's ladder, lay it against the rain gutter and climb to the roof. He would rest until the final assault to the top of the chimney. This all in itself isn't really interesting. What was interesting was that he would do this in his underwear—striped boxers with a sleeveless t-shirt and carrying with him a trumpet that he would blow from the top of the chimney, making long, straight bleeping notes over and over again. Everyone in the neighborhood would look up and muse. "Must have had a few beers." His wife would come outside and scold him, then plead for him to come down from the chimney. He would ignore her and continue with his one-note blast. She would then disappear into the house, I'm sure, embarrassed. After an hour or so, a hook-and-ladder fire truck would pull up alongside with a police patrol car, and the fireman would climb to the top of the ladder and have a conversation with the old man. The fireman would always say, "Time to come all the way down, sir." Finally, he would begin his descent, gingerly shimming down the bricks of the chimney to the roof. "Yeah, okay, the hell with it," the old man sighed. The fireman helped him down from his perch and guided him across the roof to the ladder, slipping and sliding to the oooooh's and ahhhhh's of the remaining audience. Everything seemed a lot easier going in those days.

People went back to their business and that would be the end of it. The police took the ladder away from the house and laid it down. The firemen retracted their ladder and put it back down onto the red truck. That was all. No news crews from four different television stations hanging around to film everything. BIG STORY LIVE! A pat on the back from a cop and the old man sheepishly disappeared into his back door. No problems, no worries, and that would be the end of it until next time.

In the beginning, backyard camping during the summer was what it was. Pitching a tent, getting all the bedding together, making sure you had a flashlight nearby, and making sure you were ready to do some camping after asking your parents' permission. Most of us were pros at putting the tents together from scouting. Now, we are a lot older.

A couple of us had probably kissed a girl and we were now considered veterans. Yes, athletic veterans of McKinley, Franklin and Roosevelt. We were now camping out on our own with no supervision—camping out in the backyards of friends' homes. When evening began, we started with grass throwing fights, decided who could fart the loudest, then trying to scare each other half to death before finally falling asleep. Things rapidly changed through the summer to nocturnal forays of plunder. Czech's grew large, bountiful gardens. Off we'd go, prowling around with those tiny miniature blue Morton salt shakers in our pockets. Kohlrabi and carrots, raspberries and cherries, green onions and apples, pears and plums, oh boy!

On my 13th birthday, my mother threw a small birthday party for me in our backyard. We had a little cinder block fireplace back there along with a 55-gallon drum to burn trash in. This was when the Riverside Recreation Center was popular. It was a Friday night—after the customary wieners, chips and marshmallows, we set up a large four-man military-style tent between the swing set and garage. The tent came with a canvas army cot which was placed along the back portion of the tent. My parents disappeared inside the house, knowledgeable enough to know they had just given me enough rope to hang myself.

It all started harmlessly enough, running around the yard, talking about junior high sports and general messing around. It was just more of the same until 11 p.m. That was when the hoards of people, mixed groups of boys and girls walked up the alley in groups of three or four. Somehow, the word had gotten out down at the rec center that there was a birthday party, a campout at Steve's place. Among the group of boys and girls, there was a few ninth graders who were a bit rowdy at the beginning, just a little noisy, that's all. Then I noticed a girl I recognized from my grade. She was quite a cutie pie. Then suddenly, "Hey!" yelled my father from the bedroom window. "Let's keep it down out there!" Complete silence prevailed. Everyone looked at each other with, 'Couldn't have been talking about me...' looks. The crescendo slowly rose soon after. Meanwhile, there she was, so gorgeous. She had walked up the alley from the recreation center with two of my girl classmates. I don't recall the series of events, but there we were, lying side by side on the army cot—one kiss, then two. I wasn't sure what was next, then all of a sudden my dad popped his head into the tent directly over the cot. "Hey, I thought I told you guys to…" and that's when my father looked down and saw me, his baby boy, kissing a girl. His head then disappeared and the tent flap slapped shut. "Who was that?" said the girl, sitting up looking startled. "My dad," I sighed. Knowing I was probably dead, I ran out of the tent only to see my father silently plodding across the back yard to the house in his underwear. His unannounced presence scattered everyone, including the girl I kissed. End of party. The group of merry makers continued on their routes home. My parents never mentioned a word.

EARLY INDIAN TRIBES
AND FRENCH EXPLORERS

I took the following information from many sources named in the acknowledgements of this book. Again, most of what follows are not my words.

According to an Indian legend, Iowa was named by a party of Sauk and Fox who crossed the Mississippi River in search of new hunting grounds. Impressed by the splendor of the lush, green land, their chief claimed it with his spear and enunciated something that sounded like Iowa. He then proclaimed Iowa their land. The actual source of the name, however, is still being debated. Historians are only sure that the Iowa River and the State of Iowa were named after a tribe that had nearly died out there before white people and their settlements arrived. Written forms of the name appeared in the records kept by the French, using *Ayouas, Aiouez, Ayavois;* Spanish, *Ajoues;* English, *Aiouways, Ioways.* One interpretation relates these probable misspellings to the name Auyxwa, the Dakota name for the Iowa tribe. If you say all the above words for Iowa quickly, they all sound the same or similar. The first use of the modern spelling of Iowa was on a map drawn up in 1778 by a geographer and military engineer. The first known written reference to people believed to be the Ioway occurs in an account by a French trader who, around 1656, learned from other Indians, of a river that flowed from the west into the Mississippi and of a local tribe living near it. That river is believed to be the upper Iowa River. It is likely that a trader by the name of Michael Accault first actually visited the Ioway tribe at their villages on the upper Iowa between 1677 and 1680.

Mr. Accault was interested in procuring bison hides, a roll for which the Ioway were well suited, having established hunting territories in the prairie area at the headwaters of the Upper Iowa and Cedar Rivers, and also on the lower course of the Minnesota to the north. However, by the late 1600's the Ioway abandoned their villages and migrated west along the Little Sioux and Missouri Rivers in Northwestern Iowa to be nearer to their Oto and Omaha allies. While the Ioway settled on or near the Missouri River after moving until the 1760's, they are known to have hunted throughout the territory that would later become Iowa.

The historic period began in Iowa with European exploration of the Midwest. These explorers wrote the things down that they saw and experienced. Along with leaving behind artifacts, they kept great records of when and where they were. Many Indian tribes in this area possessed and traded European goods long before they ever saw a French explorer. The historic period for these tribes began before actual contact with Europeans. In the summer of 1673, the real deal showed up. That's when the French explorers, Louis Joliet and Father Jacques Marquette traveled down the Mississippi River past the land that was to become Iowa. The two explorers, along with their five crewmen, stepped ashore near where the Iowa River flowed into the Mississippi. It is believed that the 1673 voyage marked the first time that white people visited the region of Iowa. We all know there were other people through here first; they just never chronicled it. After checking things out and surveying the surrounding area, the Frenchmen recorded in their journals that the area around there appeared to be a perfect place to settle. Other expeditions followed, and in 1682, Robert Cavalier actually reached the mouth of the Mississippi River. He claimed the entire region for France and named it Louisiana in honor of King Louis the Great.

Before 1673, however, the Iowa area had long been home to many Native American tribes. The period from the 1760's through the 1830's was a turbulent time as British and American presence in the upper Mississippi Region challenged already established French and Indian alliances. There were a lot of regional conflicts stemming out from the French and Indian war, the American Revolution and the War of 1812. This all led to the breakdown of the French fur trade and barter system the Indians depended upon, plus increased pressure and problems with American encroachment in their lands. The Sauk and Mesquaki constituted the largest and most powerful tribes in the upper Mississippi Valley.

During the early 1700's, only a few missionaries and fur traders visited the land we call Iowa, but no permanent settlements were built. In 1788, a French-Canadian Julien Dubuque bought the land from the Meskwaki to mine lead near present day Dubuque. He became the first white settler in Iowa. Soon afterwards, other settlers began to arrive. In 1803, the United States bought the entire area called Louisiana from France, which included Iowa. Two years later, the Louisiana Territory was created and the Lewis and Clark expedition was sent out to explore the new land. The Iowa Region changed into different territories as new states were created during the early 1800's. In 1821, Iowa became part of an unorganized territory of the United States. As settlers desired to move west, Native Americans were forced out of their lands.

In 1829, the Federal Government informed the Sauk and Mesquaki that they must leave their villages in Western Illinois and move across the Mississippi River into the Iowa Region. The move was made but not without violence. Chief Black Hawk, a highly respected Sauk leader, protested the move and in 1832 he went back to Illinois to reclaim his village. For the next three months, the Illinois militia pursued Chief Black Hawk and his band of approximately 400 warriors northward along the eastern side of the Mississippi. Chief Black Hawk and his warriors finally surrendered in Wisconsin with only 200 men left. This encounter was known as "The Black Hawk War." As punishment for his resistance, the government required the Sauk and Mesquaki to relinquish some of their land in eastern Iowa that they were originally forced to move to. This was known as "The Black Hawk Purchase."

The end of the Black Hawk War of 1832 gave a small area in Iowa for the first official white settlement in Iowa, which began in June 1833. Most of Iowa's first white settlers came from Ohio, Pennsylvania, New York, Indiana, Kentucky and Virginia. The Iowa territory was created on July 4, 1838. After much debate on its boundaries, Iowa became the 29th state on December 28, 1846. Over 100,000 people lived in Iowa at that time.

By 1851, all treaty lands purchased from the Indians living in Iowa was pretty much set. The Omaha, Ioway, Oto, and Missouri tribes habitated the land from the Missouri River east covering approximately one-third of the state. The Sauk and Fox area extended from there all the way to the Mississippi, except for a northern swath that was left for the Sioux. Today, Iowa is still home to one Indian tribe, the Mesquaki who reside on the Mesquaki Settlement in Tama County. (See Diagram 3.)

Diagram 3.

General map of major Native American
tribal areas in Iowa. Circa 1851.
(redrawn and simplified from Iowa State Historical Society,
Iowa City)

COLOR OF THE RIVER

CHAPTER THREE

CHAPTER THREE

Jones Park, on the southwest side of town, is located with Wilson Avenue bordering the north and Prairie Creek on the South. Teresa Drive on the west and 'C' Street on the east. Deborah Drive, Lauren Drive and Fruitland Blvd., all end into Jones Park proper. It just seemed to magically appear around 1960. I didn't realize it was even there until our family moved from 'L' Street to Deborah Drive. A girl from down the street on Deborah excitedly mentioned to me in a conspiring tone that they (the city) were going to add a swimming pool along Wilson Avenue 'really soon.' But I wasn't interested at the time. We all had Prairie Creek. Small saplings were planted along the side of the road entering Jones Park. 'Those won't last long,' I thought as I walked to a friend's house one spring. Jones Park was simply something you had to walk through to get to Prairie Creek. You must, of course, avoid the golf course and clubhouse at all cost, because for some reason, it upset the people up behind the windows of the clubhouse facing the golf course itself. They would blare through a loud speaker in angry voices. "Do not cut across the golf course. Hello, can you hear me? Remove yourselves immediately!"

By the time someone could run and jump into a cart to chase us down, we had already ran, entered our sanctuary and disappeared. Ahhhh, yes, Prairie Creek. Losing ourselves into a personal kingdom of childhood—so easy then, no worries.

One summer, a kid we hung out with had meticulously constructed a model battleship from Balsa Wood and cardboard along with a smaller vessel. The battleship was almost exactly to scale. It's super structure, the bridge, even the 16-inch guns were real looking doll sticks. Everything was perfectly detailed and painted. It was about four feet long and a foot wide. This boat was really neat looking.

The boat was built when we were eleven or twelve years old. By the time we had reached fourteen, we had grown tired of playing with it, along with our toy soldiers and plastic model airplanes. We decided to carry everything down to the creek, float the boats and bomb them from the top of the train trestle. The smaller boat went first. One guy would wade up the stream carrying the doomed craft, gently set it down in the water, and run back to climb up the trestle. We used cherry bomb firecrackers and various sized rocks. We pretended they were the enemy and we were American pilots. High over the water we waited until the first ship came into view. We made explosion sounds with our mouths when the rocks hit the water around the approaching craft with water geysers spouting up. It all appeared so real! The boat disappeared underneath us as we ran to the other side of the wooden bridge to finish it off. It sank and broke into pieces.

It was then a grand finale time for the big one. We saved most of our cherry bombs for the assault. Down the creek it came, floating towards us in elegant splendor. Long range bombs at first, arching through the air and splashing harmlessly in front and to the sides. A couple of cherry bombs flew. It came at us more swiftly now, knowing its fate and defying us. We started to panic, pelting it with everything we had and peppered it multiple times. Even more rapidly now as it slipped into the current before the trestle. We started using much large ordinance. Huge rocks rained down upon it and finally, a direct hit! It floundered and went sideways. Forget the cherry bombs, didn't have time to even light them. The battleship was still afloat, however, in distress. Under the bridge it bobbed and appeared on the other side taking on water and slowing down, then it just gently slipped under water, parts of it floating away. We watched as it went down in silence and we waited to see if it would appear again. It didn't. All that work building it. It was such a beautiful craft. Our excitement of the kill turned to sadness. Well, it was fun while it lasted.

The swift water that flowed under the train trestle was at a curve in the creek. A deep gouge had formed because of this and it was only there. We used to jump off the trestle into the water over and over again. It was very exciting when a freight train would approach. We'd wait until the last minute and then fly off into the creek 10 or 15 feet below. The engineer would blare his whistle and the guy in the caboose would shake his hand at us as they disappeared down the track.

The rest of the creek was from one foot to three feet deep, depending on where you were in the water. It seemed to get deeper as you got closer to the Cedar River. We never actually played around the outlet. It seemed dangerous, strange as it sounds. We somehow knew better and stayed away. This was a typical children's thought—better to get run over by a train than drown in the river. The wide mouth into the Cedar River was just too scary to venture around. Inner tubes were the mode of transportation in the summer and hockey skates in the winter. One couldn't stay away from down there even when it was frozen over. Ice hockey with sticks and a rock, camp fires on the bank, and just ice skating. Jones Park itself had a small pond we would ice skate on during winter. There was also a big hill at Jones Park that everyone in the neighborhood would slide and toboggan down. Families with children, big kids, little kids and then us rapscallions. We used sleds, our stomachs, cardboard, toboggans and inner tubes— it didn't matter—death defying speeds downward with absolute carnage waiting at the end.. Little kids, dogs, and small trees mowed down. With endless energy, we would run back up the hill to do it again. Winter never slowed us down, but summer at the Creek was the best. We did exploring, swimming, tries at damming it up, long talks on the banks, profound discussions about the cutest girls, most powerful firecrackers, and figuring out fractions. You're with your buddies, nothing else mattered—no cares, only the Creek. We'd spend entire days building camp sites and cutting secret stashes of firewood for the next winter. The Creek at the trestle was an open port and was shared with younger kids and older ones alike. The older boys would come down there with the girls. We would sometimes stop what we were doing and watch them interact. Nothing naughty or bad went on, just interesting for some reason, to watch and listen to them. The girls would become bored after awhile and the group would get up and leave. We would wonder, after witnessing a scene, what it was all about. Even though none of us, as far as I knew, ever took a girl down there. I think I know. They were probably four or five years older than us, but still playful kids at heart and wanted their girlfriends to experience the same 'something' they had before. The girls weren't 'kids at heart' and missed the 'why we are down here' thing. The guys would jump and dive into the water. They would splash around and mimic drowning. The girls kept their 'when can we leave' look on all the time. I hated those girls and felt sorry for the guys. However, dupe-dee-do, off we'd go forgetting about them and chop some trees down to build another camp. We explored the confluence of Prairie Creek and Cedar River as far back up the Creek to Hawkeye Downs. Little did we know that it flowed past Atkins, Iowa and finally dissipated somewhere west of Van Horne. It might be nice, one day, to take an inner tube ride from the headwaters of Prairie Creek into the Cedar.

When the Jones Park swimming pool finally opened, I was there and probably the first guy in line. I used to swim at Ellis. It was the place to be. Now we had a pool of our own right in our neighborhood. With a rough estimate of approximately 10,000 kids around, it was an instant hit. I was right on the ground level. Well, me and the girl who had first become excited about the new swimming pool. What a beauty she was, and I had no idea where my mind was during that time. She used to write notes to me, right on my t-shirt while I was wearing it, as I waited in line for the doors to open. I was such an idiot. The swimming pool at Jones Park was the coolest. The aroma of suntan lotion, chlorine and the snack bar were in the air. Lots of girls, my friends and I, hot days with sunny skies. It was hard to stay contained. Prairie Creek was forgotten for a while. One of my friends' older sister worked at the pool handing out heavy safety pins with a number stamped on a tag at the end to pin onto your swimwear. This pin corresponded to a portal on the swimming pool side and your clothing was stored on shelves where you could retrieve your personal things later.

The sister was cute, the lifeguards were cute, girls swimming at the pool were cute. Paradise! Jones Park swimming pool, 1960. Prairie Creek had faded so far in the past that I couldn't believe it. I joined the lifesaving classes, the swim team, and even the synchronized swim team. I couldn't wait to get over to the pool during summer. I literally lived there with morning classes and afternoon goofing around in the pool. It closed at 9 p.m., and the parking lot was grid locked with older guys with cars scoping things out, parents picking up their kids, and us, just meandering around wondering where to go next. Lots of activity at the end of the pool day. Jones Park pool had a swim team and we were pretty bad in the beginning. The swim coach was great and dedicated. He just didn't have any talent available for him to help the team along. He was our life saving class instructor and with another young woman, our synchronized swimming coach. I was easily talked into the synchronized swim club because I had no idea what synchronized swimming even was. I did know it meant more time at the pool. We were so bad at synchronization and coordination that our coaches decided to turn us into a clown act instead.

We had two small neighborhood performances during programs between swim races before disbanding. Our swim team was a coed team with quite a large group of 9 to 10, 11 to 12, and 13-14-year olds. The coach selected which kids from each age group would swim, what strokes, and what distances. I was taught the breaststroke, and it became my specialty in the 50-yard and 100-yard individual and all relays. We usually were slaughtered by the other city teams, especially Ellis. They had some flyers. Jones Park team would join with other swimmers from Cedar Rapids and we would travel to places like Marion, Muscatine and Clinton to compete. Only the 13 to 14-year old age group would go on trips and the Jones pool coach would drive us in his car to the swim meets where we would hook up with other competitors from Cedar Rapids. Road trips—it was so adult. Cedar Rapids met visiting teams at Ellis Pool because it was the largest. I wasn't a very good racer and had a difficult time staying in my swim lane. I had a good time though and even came in second place once. Life saving classes were different, and it was serious stuff. To enter into a class you had prerequisites to perform. You had to be able to swim 200 yards non-stop and swim 50 yards underwater. Then you were approved to begin training. In order to pass the course and receive your life saving certificate, you had to follow the correct procedures to rescue someone, which involved basic maneuvers to complete. As a final test, you had to pull the 200 lb., six-foot tall coach 50 yards to safety while he fought with you all the way. Of course, there was the CPR and mouth-to-mouth resuscitation and to make sure the airways were opened. We all passed. My summers at Prairie Creek and Jones Park were bliss.

At the same time as my Prairie Creek and Jones Park adventures, there was, of course, things going on during school at Wilson Junior High. Wilson's teachers, staff and coaches alike didn't put up with anything. The worst anyone did in Junior High during that time was talking in class, stuffing someone into a locker, or gum chewing. Alcohol, drugs or even cigarettes were unheard of. My how things change. There was a football coach at Wilson who used to express himself and get a point across using the Czech language. "Damn it, keep your prdel down when blocking!" Stuff like that—with every sentence at practice. Intimidating to a 13 or 14-year old. I was so used to hearing Czech words, throughout my school years. I didn't realize that they weren't part of the English language. He tried to shape up and teach kids the fundamentals of football. He always wore a white t-shirt in health class or PE classes. He was solid, fair and real, and he could crush you with just a look. I was an equipment manager (water boy) for the Wilson Ramblers. There were three of us, all too small to play Junior High football or detasle corn for that matter, but we were there at every practice and game time, scraping mud off the squad's cleats and handing out water bottles during timeouts. We made sure all the helmets, shoulder pads, pants and jerseys were ready every day. You didn't mess with coach. You made sure everything was in order or suffer the wrath. There was absolutely no swearing either, only he was allowed to swear and used his right. He is one of the reasons kids make it through life—early discipline and respect.

Going steady with a girl was a big thing, sort of like a status symbol. Junior high school girls and boys having a special or significant other. The girls were showing off their newly acquired friendship rings worn on necklaces around their necks or wrapped on the bottom with angora darn and worn on a tiny finger. Wilson smelled like a school—the wax on the floors and hallways, the old varnished wood in the classrooms, and the smell of the gymnasium. This was my brother Larry's high school. Wilson was famously better known as Czech Tech. I was surprised to see it still looked identical to when my friends and classmates were enrolled and walked those very halls. Across 'J' Street S.W. was an older-style grocery store with front steps to walk up to the entrance. All I can remember the store selling was candy and soft drinks. I suppose it sold grocery items like a 7-Eleven, but all I remember is the large variety of candies and snacks. What else would you need to sell being across the street from a junior high school. It was the place to hang out after school. You had to at least stop by just to find out what had transpired during the school day when there were no athletic practices going on. Students were on the sidewalk out front, the cement stairway and loitering around outside of the store. Not only was it a social event, but that's where all the gossip was—who was currently going steady with who and who had broken up with who and available, what took place in third period social studies and girls whispering about who didn't have to dress for gym class. Everything could be learned about that particular day's activities in the classrooms and hallways. Fights between guys were usually held out front. "Oh yeah, I'll see you across the street," which was met with, "You're chicken to show up!" Conversations along that line. I can still see the woman's face behind the counter. She had bright reddish hair but I can't seem to remember her name or the people who owned that small store. The building is still sitting there almost looking much like it did back then. Anyway, that red-haired lady fit right in with the rest of us. Just as silly as we were and full of tricks and teasing, I guess you had to be able to deal with young kids. She seemed genuinely happy to see everyone in the afternoon.

There was another small store and gas station on the corner of Wilson and Bowling Street S.W. called the 'Hilltop.' Along with the store was an older-style trailer park that extended back from the end of the store. I'd been inside the small store plenty of times before on my way home from practice and with my dad stopping by for a couple of gallons of gas and a loaf of bread on our way home from some place or another. My dad also delivered ice cream there. The man who owned the store lived four or five houses down from us on Deborah Drive and so knew our family. One day when I was in the store, he asked if I'd like a job there stocking shelves, sweeping up and pumping gas during the summer months. Wow, a job! I wonder what that's like. A friend and I had picked strawberries west of town and cleaned the trash from underneath the bleachers at Hawkeye Downs before, but this was a real job. My parents thought it would be a good idea, so I accepted the job. I had no idea what it took to be employed—the regimen, the minor sacrifices, and above all the responsibility. No more Prairie Creek, Jones Park Pool and messing around with friends. My first job—I showed up every day and performed my duties as best I could. After a few 'explanations' from the boss, I got relatively straightened out about what I was actually supposed to do and why. The owner had a nephew or family member who was the original stocker before me and he's the one who trained me. He had gotten older and had another job lined up, so he was moving on. This kid owned the neatest old coupe I'd seen to that point. I can't recall what make or year it was, but it was shiny black and clean with a longer than normal engine compartment. When I was 15, he had stopped by the store to see the boss and as I was admiring it, he asked if I'd like to drive it home for lunch since he had some things to do, and needed to stay awhile. (The family maintained a large apartment on the Wilson Avenue side of the store.) I was elated and luckily knew how to drive a stick shift. Off I went at lunchtime, heading home—afraid and ecstatic at the same time. "Mom, Mom, look!" I shouted as I ran up to the front door. "Yes, that's a nice car…a little old isn't it?" she smiled. Oh well, I thought it was cool. Anyway, I always thought highly of that kid. He let me drive it out of pure kindness. Yes, I was alone to take care of the store, to pass each chicken egg over a bare light bulb and place it into a dozen container, sweep up the outside and when all the stocking and dusting was done, I would retire to a small building out back and separate what seemed to be two or three million empty soda bottles into every different manufacturer's container. How the poor owner put up with me I'll never know. I wasn't the brightest kid on the block; he was pretty affable with a good sense of humor. It seems he was always smiling like he already knew I was going to screw up and that was okay. It was years later, many years later that I found out he was Syrian—from an immigrant family perhaps. No, the King's English was spoken perfectly. It made me think, what are Middle Eastern families doing in Cedar Rapids? As I remembered and recalled more things about my family after that, I realized my mom and dad knew another family who was also of Arab descent. I can remember this one man and his family. One evening back in the late 1940's when I was around four years old, we were visiting this family at their home. I had a bad habit of sucking my thumb at that time. I would carry with me my little blanket that I would press against my cheek. My parents tried a lot of different methods to try and make me stop, but nothing worked. On this particular evening, my dad's friend said to me, "Hey, Steve, come here a minute. Since you like to suck on your thumb so much, I'll put a little sweetener on it to make it taste better, okay?" My father was sitting at the kitchen table with him, so I thought nothing wrong. It was red in color and turned out to be some sort of hot pepper that burned the heck out of my mouth. I cried and complained bitterly to no avail. Nothing was done and I was angry with everyone for quite some time, especially him. Years passed and he always teased me about that incident. My anger diminished as I became older. He owned a service station down on 'E' Avenue and Ellis Boulevard in later years. Mike and I stopped by the station one time before he passed away. We wanted to see him and say 'Hello.' He walked out of the office, saw who we were and a big smile appeared on his face. He recognized us, and yes, it was good. We hugged, shook hands, patted each other on the back, and you could see on his face how happy it made him to see his old pal's kids.

When I was in high school cruising down a tree-lined street with an island median separating the street, I would sometimes notice these ladies tending to the flower gardens on the wide medians. Catholic nuns? Maybe something else. Wrapped in blue flowing robes with white veils across their faces, who were these ladies, I thought. Some sort of religious group of people or something. Oh well, and on I drove, naive and oblivious to everything.

Arabs came to America because of severe economic conditions, restrictive government policies on certain ethnic groups or religious freedoms being curtailed in their native countries—the same reasons European, Hispanic, and Asian immigrants came. Why the Midwest and Cedar Rapids in particular? Inexpensive farmland and wide-open spaces. Lebanese Christians and Muslims together were the first to arrive in the Cedar Rapids area in the late 1880's. Communities such as Des Moines, Waterloo and most important, Ft. Dodge, where a fellow named Habaab and his brothers held the satisfaction of being the first Muslims to settle in the state of Iowa some time between 1880 and 1888. Because of the fine, rich farmland, some became farmers. They bypassed major population centers explicitly for the open space available to them. Muslim immigrants in Cedar Rapids numbered about 45 by 1914. Mostly single men, they hoped to earn enough money to be able to return home and find good Muslim wives. Most of the new arrivals began the same way as their predecessors, as back peddlers. Slowly they made the transition to traveling salesmen and small shop owners. The farmers became providers of butter, eggs and other farm products to the city population with the help of the peddlers and salesmen, who, through time, had earned enough money to buy horses and buggies and then later on purchase small trucks.

Muslims helping Muslims—and because of the tolerance and acceptance they found here, continued growing. It always amazed me how immigrants introduced to a new and different culture can thrive without speaking the native language and having to learn new living styles, let alone the different foods. By the mid-1920's, Cedar Rapids, which of all the cities in the area, finally attracted the largest number of Muslims. They could claim more than 50 shops and grocery stores owned and operated by Arabs. Muslims had been gathering together for communal prayer during the early years and in 1918 decided to form a group to actually build a Mosque of their own. By 1925, this group called themselves the 'Rose of Fertility' lodge, and later in 1929, they hired from the old country the equivalent of a priest or reverend called an Imam, to conduct services. This was when they finally were serious about building a proper Mosque. After much hard work and preparation, the Mosque was completed in 1934 and an open house was held there. Yes, the first Muslim Mosque built in North America was right here in Cedar Rapids, Iowa. It should be noted that an earlier Mosque was built in 1929 in Ross, South Dakota, Edmonton, Canada, and Brooklyn, New York. These Mosques were just buildings called Mosques. A real Mosque needs to have the proper classic Islamic architectural style. You can't have a room above a restaurant or grocery store and have it as a proper mosque. Our mosque in Cedar Rapids is called the 'Mother Mosque of North America.' The first one right here in River City is still standing. It seems that the more I get into the history of this stuff, the more proud I am about Cedar Rapids. While planning to build a larger Mosque to accommodate the growing Muslim community around 1970, the mother mosque was sold to finance a new one. The old mosque was used as a teen center during that time and then it became a Christian Pentecostal church and then later abandoned in the late 1980's. Then it was up for sale again. In

1990, the Islamic Council of Iowa repurchased the building and began renovation and restoration to bring it to its original condition. In 1992, a grand opening was held along with local dignitaries and it is now on the National Register of Historic Places. I grew up with a few or more of these people that were Arabs on the southwest side, and I didn't even know it. I thought they were all Czech, but of course, in grade school, I thought everyone was Czech. The mother mosque in Cedar Rapids is located at 1335 9th Street, N.W.

I've taken the liberty to recount the following history of Cedar Rapids from multiple publications and authors named in the acknowledgment section of this writing, again, some verbatim.

Although there is no written history, the Cedar River was probably well known to early English and French trappers, hunters and adventurers—following it back up from the Mississippi to the Iowa and then camping along the Cedar River banks. We know that the Cedar Rapids area was occupied by roving bands of Sax and Fox, Sioux, Meskwaki and Winnebago Indians who savored the valley of the Cedar River as a beautiful, peaceful place and who, after a while, relinquished it without a fight. It's better to just move along. We also know that the first person of European blood to settle permanently in what is now Cedar Rapids was a man named Osgood Shepherd. Mr. Shepherd has been called 'colorful'—a professional hunter and trapper, but better known as a 'horse trader.' In 1837 he built a cabin on the corner of First Avenue and First Street, N.E. This first structure in Cedar Rapids was apparently a hangout for horse thieves, and also served as a tavern.

Today, a 60-foot landmark 'Tree of Five Seasons' is the spot that the cabin stood. Later that same year, a fellow named William Stone showed up and staked a claim nearby, but was threatened, harassed and driven across the river to the west side by Mr. Shepherd—not an ideal founding father. Some historians believe it was Mr. Stone who actually made the first claim and not Mr. Shepherd.

William Stone came to the area to trade with local Indians and staked a claim where Wilson and Company used to stand, and it was Mr. Shepherd who jumped Stone's claim. Alas, by 1839, other folks started showing up and started settling here. By 1841, gristmills and Sawmills were in operation turning the area settlement into a trade center and later known as a primary grain-milling center. In the late 1830's and early 1840's, flat-bottom boats about 50 feet long floated grain and other products down the river. At one point there were not only flatboats, but also the keel boats popularized by Disney in the 'Mike Fink' series on television along with various different types of barges that all navigated the Cedar River when high waters made it possible. In 1842 the nickname 'Rapids City' was given to the settlement and the first frame house was erected. That summer, the first large riverboat to come to 'Rapids City' was the 'Maid of Iowa.' It was a steam-powered boat built in Iowa and owned by the Mormon leader, Joseph Smith. It carried Mormon settlers and cargo. After that, the steamboat went up the river to Waterloo. Later the boat came down and left for St. Louis loaded with grain. It was supposed to come back to Cedar Raids for another load, but never returned. By 1844, brick buildings were built, and in 1847, the first schoolhouse and a post office were erected. In 1847, the University of Iowa was founded in Iowa City. The town was resurveyed in 1848 and incorporated under a town charter. The name of the town was called Cedar Rapids and in 1849, Martin L. Barber was selected as the first mayor of the city. Some time during this period, the town of Kingston, located on the west side of the river, was started and was a separate entity from Cedar Rapids. Both cities grew alongside each other and Kingston was finally annexed to Cedar Rapids in 1870. The first newspaper and the first church were built in 1850. In 1851, COE College was founded and the population had expanded to 380 people. In 1855, the village of Amana was started southwest of town. In 1856, the first bridge to span the Mississippi River was built at Davenport. In 1858, the population had risen to 1400 souls. The railroad reached Cedar Rapids in 1859, which hastened the demise of the riverboats used for commerce. The last large steamer to run in Cedar Rapids was around 1866. Eventually, the Federal Government deemed the Cedar River 'unnavigatable' because of its shifting sandbars and shallow depths—just too dangerous.

Iowa has always been a progressive state. In 1820, the Missouri Compromise made Iowa a non-slave area, so before the Civil War, the state was overwhelmingly against slavery.

Iowa provided 75,797 white solders, five sailors and marines and 440 black soldiers in nine Calvary regiments, four light artillery batteries, 45 infantry regiments and two infantry battalions to the Union

Army. My great, great grandfather, Nathan Brown, on my mom's side of the family, fought in the war for the North. The 14th, 15th, and 24th Iowa infantry regiments had men from the Cedar Rapids and Linn County area, with the County Court House in Marion serving as the enlistment point for Union volunteers. A total of 337 officers and 13,252 enlisted Iowans died as a result of the war. Many times this number of soldiers were wounded or maimed in battle. In 1868, black men received the right to vote in Iowa. At the end of the war, people flowed into Cedar Rapids. Housing, stores, factories and machine shops were constructed. Cedar Rapids had become a city.

COLOR OF THE RIVER

CHAPTER FOUR

CHAPTER FOUR

Williams Blvd. S.W. to Highway 151, they are both one in the same. All the way, southwest to the small town of Fairfax, Iowa. If you continued on 151, you will hit the Amana Colonies. At Fairfax, there was an old abandoned quarry full of water and waiting for us. High limestone cliffs at 90-degree angles on the north, south and west sides. You could drive down on the sloping north side to the water where the slope came down to a three-foot rocky ledge, then on a few yards more to the water's edge and a rocky beach. Along the west cliff, the water was deep. We would spend all day at the quarry on weekends during the summers of 1962 and 1963—a perfect summer teenage spot. For some reason or another, hardly any locals hung out there. We basically had it to ourselves. I can't remember who found it. Clean, clear water, a ten- or twenty-acre natural swimming pool, with a large parking lot for our automobiles at the bottom near the water. Fairfax Quarry was used only during daylight hours. A little too scary at night, and besides, the sheriff's deputies would show up when we started up a campfire. Daylight was the best time—cooling off under the hot Iowa sun and humidity. Cut-off blue jeans were the tout ensemble of choice. The girls added a bathing suit top to their attire. Running leaps off the cliffs and then climbing dangerously back up the rocks just to launch ourselves again was great.

Cheers and jeers came from the opposite side where the cars were parked. People still swimming in the water below the cliff, desperately trying to avoid being landed upon. At times, we would try to hit the center of the inner tube of a tractor tire floating below. The thought of splitting our heads open or snapping bones never entered our minds. Later on we acquired a raft made from 55-gallon drums, 2x4's and plywood. It had a living room rug nailed to the top and it was beautiful. I can't remember if we built it or someone else did and left it floating alone. Now we had a platform to float around on and dive off from. We would take large stones out onto the raft and use them as a means to sink rapidly to the muddy bottom just to find out how deep the quarry was. There was this one guy who swore he had touched the top of some machinery down on the bottom. The girls would only come with us on occasion. We'd usually ignore them while performing our stunts, rough housing around and doing other silly things associated with being a teenaged boy. Very rarely would the girls get into the water with us. They would just sit on the blankets or car hoods and talk among themselves and occasionally glance over at our antics. It's no wonder they wouldn't jump into the water with us—as often as we'd try to pretend to drown them. I still don't understand why high school girls put up with high school boys. We were a nice group of guys and everything as relative gentlemen would be; however, most of us were dumber than the mud we clomped around in while wearing moronic grins.

In 1963, towards the end of summer, one of our guys in the group joined the Navy. We held a kegger in his honor at the quarry. It was a going-away party that became way too fun, that while we were down below in a flat area hooting and howling in the late afternoon, the cops came. Two sheriff deputy cruisers with lights flashing raced in from on top of the cliffs. They had us…no way out…our only escape blocked. "Hide me!" the Navy kid rasped loudly. "I can't get caught, the Navy won't let me in." What to do…What to do? Our seventeen-year-old minds overloaded with dilemma. "Get in the trunk..hurry, get in, get in!" "Yeah, okay, okay, good!" as he climbed in trying to find room for his long legs.

"Me too, me too! his cousin chimed in.

"Let him in," the Navy guy said, trying to make more room where there was none. For some reason, none of us ever found out, the cousin apparently had some sort of problem going on with the police.

"Okay, gees, get in…get in, hurry up!" we said, stuffing him down and slamming the trunk shut on them. Then acting like nothing at all had happened, we drove up to the road block at the entrance to the main road out of the quarry. We followed behind a virtual caravan of automobiles.

"Everybody out," one deputy said sternly walking back towards our car carrying a large flashlight in his hand after letting the first two cars through. "Open the trunk, please," he said gesturing up with the flashlight. He didn't even ask for identification. "What's going on," he said to no one in particular while peering into the trunk at our friends stuffed inside.

"Ahhh, nothing really. We were just leaving." After lining everybody up, the officer politely asked why the two guys were in the trunk of the automobile. Everyone stared at their feet in silence. The cousin tried to become invisible. The Navy kid stood up straight and began to clearly explain everything.

"And you, what's your story?" The policeman said to the Navy guy's cousin. He started to blabber something that didn't make sense.

"He's with me, we joined the Navy together," the enlistee offered.

"That's right?" the cop asked.

"Yes, sir," the cousin answered.

They searched the cars for alcohol, confiscated any loose bottles they found and sent us on our way shouting, "It's too dangerous down there to be boozing it up. Okay, that's it, no more, you won't get off so easily next time, understand!"

"Yes sir, thank you sir. Thank you," was our grateful reply. Whew, just had the hell scared out of us. Everyone in the car stayed silent until we were out of town and heading home. As we got closer to Cedar Rapids, it all became a big joke and we started laughing about it. Things were a lot more easy going back then. Nowadays, we would all have been cited and in court with DUI's, drinking underage, public drunkenness, or a hundred other offenses. Subconsciously, we must have retained the warning, I can't remember ever going back down to the quarry at Fairfax.

The Red Cedar River flooded. I think it was around spring 1961. Riverside Park was mostly under water. A call went out to the citizens of Cedar Rapids to help with sandbags. Either fill them, load them, drop them off, or join a sandbag crew to form a dike. The people of Cedar Rapids responded. A classmate of mine borrowed the flatbed truck from his father's business and three or four of us headed towards Ellis Park. We had stopped first at the Cedar Rapids Department of Public Works. I believe they called it the City Barns between 4th and 5th Ave. on 1st Street S.W. where there were people frantically filling bags of sand. We loaded up the truck and headed towards Ellis. We ran into a group of Army Reserve soldiers who apparently had just finished building a sandbag dike along Ellis Blvd. right where you first enter the park. Ellis Blvd. went straight on into the park where the flooding river was on the right and either Ellis Lane or 'Q' Avenue went left. The soldiers walked back down the boulevard to a couple of troop trucks about two blocks away. A large guy with short blonde hair stayed behind and told us to, "Build a barrier right here on Ellis Lane, and don't move!" The soldier who told us that must have been the boss, a sergeant or something.

"And every hour I want you to check over the side of the sandbags and see if the water is rising in this area or not; and come tell me if it does, got it!" he ordered. We were good soldiers and did exactly as he said. Around 3 a.m., we heard a police car come speeding up Ellis Blvd. It screeched to a halt next to the reservist and I saw the Sergeant point towards me and my buddies. Oh no! We scrambled around our mini fort, bumping into each other and looking over the back side of our sandbag wall to see if any water might have risen. Elated to find no water had crept up on us anywhere, we began shouting, "There's no water coming up here! Everything's okay!" At that, the police officer revved his cruiser and headed towards us anyway. He slid to a stop, "Get in," he shouted.

"What, we didn't do anything."

"Get in the car, we need you guys on the other side," he explained. Off we went past the Army guys who were now climbing into their truck with the siren on, "It's coming over the sandbags at Quaker Oats," he said. "And we need everybody we can get to help." Fifteen minutes later, all of us were up to our waist in the water, handing sandbags from one to the other. There must have been 15 or 20 of us that joined the already beleaguered men and women that had been working in that area all that night. We finished building the protective dike right before the sun came up and we hitched a ride back to my friend's truck. On the way home, we stopped at a Red Cross lunch wagon that was handing out baloney sandwiches, hot coffee and sugar cookies. We gobbled it down and profusely thanked the two elderly ladies who also worked the entire night feeding everyone they could.

I'm traveling on Highway 30 towards Clinton, Iowa with three high school friends. It was the summer of 1962, and we were headed for Cordova, Illinois to witness the world series of drag racing—going to cross the Mississippi River at Clinton and then head south to Cordova. There was something that was always in the Iowa air—a comfortable, natural smell—the scent of country. It was everywhere, heavy and muggy. The thick aroma of mown hay and manure with a hint of pesticide combined altogether. Dark rows of corn flying by like a long-legged man running crazily beside us in the black soil, trying to keep up, his corn row legs almost a blur. An ocean of green, fertile farmland stretching over rolling hills, corn growers for the entire world, white grain silos off in the distance. A gray dust spray bellowing behind some fast-moving object traveling parallel to us on an unseen road. An occasional miller moth popping against the windshield in a yellow puff. The sun was behind us and the quiet evening lay ahead in a hot sticky haze. We managed to acquire a case of Falstaff. The old kind of beer case constructed of sturdy cardboard where the top folded down into the middle from both sides. Each glass bottle had its own individual holder to separate all 24 containers. These cases would keep ice frozen almost forever. I believe we drank alcohol not only to maintain our camaraderie and bolster our enthusiasm, but also to curb our apprehension about what lay ahead.

None of us had ever been out of the state on our own before. This trip was brand new stuff, and it was kind of spooky crossing over the bridge. What was on the other side waiting for us? Border guards, bandits maybe—of course not, ridiculous. When you were a kid and your parents traveled out of state, you never paid attention. You now are on your own. Oh, oh, the bridge is coming to an end. Road signs ahead. This is too quick, we're in Illinois already! A little panicky, we're not quite sure which lane to be in.

"Which way do I go, huh, which way?" the driver asked.

"Follow the signs, just follow the signs south."

"Where, what signs?"

"Here, turn here!" someone yelled.

We arrived unprepared in a foreign place.

"Yeah, yeah, stay in this lane, there's the route we need."

Everyone alert, eyes wide, safely across and on the correct course south bound. Looks a lot like Iowa over here, smells the same too. Not so scary anymore, and we continued along taking in the sights. Can't see the river anymore, but that's all right. After about 30 minutes of driving, we happened upon a series of roadside stands selling cantaloupe, t-shirts, soda, and anything else you could imagine. It was getting dark and we could tell we were almost there. This was a big thing for teenagers; our excitement was building. The world series of drag racing at Cordova, Big Daddy Don Garlits, Connie Kaletta, the big names at the time in the drag racing world. There were also a couple of guys from Cedar Rapids we actually knew that was racing.

Zero to 180 mph in six seconds—spectacular and electrifying—the smell of nitro and burning rubber, the roar from spectators, all the different-colored shapes and styles of the hot rods revving their engines and accelerating off the starting line. It was thrilling exhilaration, couldn't wait.

We decided before leaving Cedar Rapids that we would arrive the night before the semi-finals and spend the night somewhere near the raceway, ready for the next morning's activities. We were so clever with brilliant thinking—why pay for a camping site in the accompanying lots available nearby? We would pull over someplace and do a little unauthorized camping in our automobile. Gee whiz, it didn't take a brain surgeon to figure that out. We drove past a large entry area that was brightly lit with an enormous banner over the entrance proclaiming the '1962 World Series of Drag Racing' with the National Hot Rod Association logos and other sponsored advertisements. We could see the racing cars parked everywhere inside the pit areas and beyond, the empty bleachers. There was a lot of activity going on inside the gates. We didn't find a good place to pull over and park until we drove further south into the outskirts of a small town down the highway. The next morning wasn't pretty. Mosquito-bitten, sticky, sweaty, hung over and dry-mouthed, we found out the small town was called Port Byron. Of course, we didn't think to bring a change of clothes or toothbrushes or anything at all for that matter. We had become more interested in getting that case of beer for the trip. We didn't need anything else. Just gas money...just gas money?

"Hey, how much money does anybody have?" dead silence.

"Wadya mean?" a voice asked.

"You know, spending money." There was more silence, everyone looking at one another with blank stares.

"I have some extra, but you'll have to pay me back," one guy said.

"Me too," I said.

After financial arrangements were made, everyone had enough after putting our dollars and change together. All day admission fees, parking, some food, and most important, beer money. Not a lot of cash, but enough.

The drag races at Cordova were everything we expected, but at a much slower pace. We were seated in the stands near the starting area—a perfect spot. We were enjoying ourselves when about an hour into it, suddenly a Circa 1930's Fiat coupe, screaming off the start line in a blue cloud of burning tires, actually exploded in front of our eyes. Parts of the engine went flying everywhere like a discharged hand grenade causing a ducking reflex from the crowd. The car crashed into a retaining wall twenty feet away from us with a loud scraping, tearing sound, and pieces flying off of the car body sending what was left of the racer back out onto the track with only the seat compartment and roll bar left unscathed, which rolled over and over down the asphalt scattering debris and then finally spinning to a smoking stop. Everything was now on fire. Death! Sixteen years old and I just witnessed someone dying. It was a sickening chill that enveloped me, my eyes glued to the fiery cockpit area that was left. Pit crews and fire control people with fire extinguishers rushed up to the wreck and covered everything with white foam.

The entire area was now surrounded with emergency personnel who were trying to extract whatever was left of the driver. I heard cheering and thought, 'My God, how sick is that. What's wrong with these people? Then I saw why. The driver was standing up and waving at the crowd. He removed his helmet and nonchalantly walked over to an ambulance that was waiting. No way could that guy have walked away from something that devastating, no way. The event recharged us, so back to the beer stand we went. Adult entertainment! By the early evening the hot rods were still darting off the starting line like roaring jet planes. We were starting to fade and tired of the repeating noise level. Too much sun and beer contributed to our weariness. We bought a couple of air-brushed hot rod t-shirts and a cantaloupe to split as we walked back to the car. We then realized that we needed to find a place to sleep again and drove out of the parking area. We followed other exiting traffic south towards Moline. The next day was Sunday, and the finals. One of our crew had gotten a bit too inebriated during the day and began asking us to pull over.

"Oh man, you guys, I'm getting sick. Pull over, hurry, right now!" he begged. Watching him vomit through his fingers wasn't nice. It sprayed everywhere as we stepped back. Pieces of orange cantaloupe stuck to the front of his brand new puke-soaked shirt. He was a drooling mess. We couldn't do anything with him; he just lay beside the car while we stood watching him with apprehension.

"Let's leave him," someone joked.

"Nooooo," he responded, raising his arm in protest.

"I'm okay...okay?" he pleaded.

So we stuffed him back in the car. A rancid sort of fermented odor emanated from the back seat as we continued on our way. We found our old 'camping' spot from the night before and retired there for the night.

A very bright light illuminated us from somewhere outside as it cast sharp shadows in the interior of the automobile. Then there were two or three quick taps on the driver's side window. "Hello in there, wake up!" It was an authoritative, yet ethereal voice. Where was it coming from?

"Hey, open up, let's go!"

Apparently, some time had passed since we pulled over as everyone was slow to acknowledge, but pulled it together enough to reply with something like, "Huh?"

"Everybody out!" the voice said. Cops, we thought. After explaining our situation to the Port Byron police and then them checking our identifications and automobile registration, we were told to move on.

"You're going to have to find a spot back at the campground, can't park along the highway here boys... okay?"

"Yes sir, okay."

Off we went heading back north still feeling the effects of the day festivities.

"Are they still following us?"

"Yeah."

"Wanna just keep going?"

"You mean all the way home?"

"I don't know, what do you guys think?"

My own bed and a hot shower sounded real good.

"But, we'll miss the finals tomorrow."

"Yeah, but, gees…are the cops still behind us?"

"Nah, they must have turned off."

We drove past the entrance to the speedway, and nobody said a word. We silently crossed back over the bridge into Iowa. At least our foreign license plates wouldn't stand out anymore. Following the route signs into Clinton proper, as there were no four lanes back then. That's when we came upon a small delay. Two young girls were sitting out on a front porch wearing short shorts and sleeveless blouses.

They were cute, 14 or 15 years old with big smiles and waving to us as we drove slowly down the wide deserted street. It was 1 a.m. in the morning.

"Stop the car, go back!" I said. "Did you see them, huh, did you?" I slobbered. I became adamant; my friends stopped, turned around and drove back to the house. We pulled up to the curb. It was a large, older wood frame with a large front porch and wide steps. It was a two-story wood frame home with a covered porch extending out. Above the porch were two windows, one on each side of the apex of the house. The porch below was enclosed on each end with wooden lattice work. After a brief conversation from the car window, I got out, embolden with alcohol, walked right up to the girls. They were really pretty—I'm not kidding. They could have possibly been sisters, and they were cutie pies straight from heaven. I sat with both of them and after a few minutes, we began with some suggestive teasing, the younger one seemed to be the leader of the two. I forgot all about my friends waiting for me since

I had other things on my mind. After kissing her, she suggested I go upstairs with her and 'talk awhile.' She told me that I couldn't go through the house because she was afraid that her parents would awaken. I climbed up the lattice work to the roof of the porch and effortlessly crawled over to look in the lighted window. The girls were both in the upstairs bedroom giggling and whispering between themselves, as they were making up a double bed with hurried seriousness on their faces. The younger girl that I was now in love with, changed into a nighty that stretched tightly across her body as she bent over to straighten the top blanket. She then smiled through the window as she approached to let me in. I glanced down the street one last time and saw that the car was gone—it had disappeared somewhere. Who cares—I'll hitchhike home.

"Hey you, you on the roof!" Startled, I looked down and across the street stood a drunkard or bum holding onto a street sign with his other arm outstretched and pointing straight at me. "Get down from there," he said. Leaning forward to focus on me again. The bedroom immediately became dark and the window stayed shut. I tried to lay flat and ignore the drunk's protest, but he continued. "Whatcha doing up there, get down."

I squeezed my eyes shut. I couldn't believe it. What else could go wrong, and just like a Hollywood script, a patrol car drove by and the vagrant flagged the police down. He leaned over into the passenger side of the police car window for a moment and then the driver looked up and saw me.

"All right buddy, come on down." The policeman then got out of his police cruiser. I hesitated.

"Now," he said. Okay, now I'm dead. I clambered down to the ground and walked over to the policeman's car and immediately began babbling. They dismissed the bum, and he saundered on down the sidewalk happy to have done his civic duty.

"Okay, slow down a little bit," I must have sounded incoherent. The officers listened with surprising interest, glancing at the house intermittently. I explained everything from start to finish and didn't make anything up or lie.

"So, where's your friends right now?" the officer asked.

I looked around. "Gee, I don't know. I don't think they would leave me."

"Hop in the car, we'll have a look around."

"Ahhh, okay." Off we went down the street, slowly patrolling the neighborhood. The driver looked over at his partner and said, "I think somebody in this car has been drinking."

"Not me," the other officer said. Then both of them fell silent again. They finally spotted someone walking towards us on the opposite sidewalk holding a blanket that was mostly dragging behind him. It was the kid in the puke-smelling t-shirt, and he appeared to be in bad shape. This is exactly what I didn't want them to see. When my buddy saw the police car, he froze.

"Is this one of your missing friends?"

"Yeah," I said quietly.

"Come on over here son, you okay?" My friend wilted a bit and then walked over to the car like walking to a firing squad.

"Yeah, I'm okay," he answered. Then he saw me in the back seat and his eyebrows perked up and a smile fell across his face. Then it must have hit him, I was arrested, something bad happened with the girls and we were all going to jail. His smile faded, face forlorn. Just then, our car came up the block, slowed down and then saw us and stopped.

"These your buddies?"

"Yeah."

"Okay, time to get this straightened out." After talking to each of us individually, the police cut us loose. Apparently, that particular house and the two girls were well known to the local constablatory and believed our story.

Policemen have a tendency to already know the truth about what really took place in most situations and what's generally going on while working their beat areas. I learned something that night about lying and also about having good friends. If you ever get caught doing something, no matter how bad you think it might be for you, confess, especially to the police. You'll usually get cut loose and won't spend time looking over your shoulder. Of course, our identification and auto registration was again being checked. Then we were sternly told to, "Leave the area boys, and go home."

The police followed us to the Clinton city limits and sent us packing down the lonely highway. We all made it home that morning and fell into our beds. I felt sorry for the last guy who had to drive home alone.

Friday evenings, Saturdays and mostly Sunday afternoons, we were in cruising mode. First it was my mom's 1958 Oldsmobile 88. This was before my stepfather bought me a two-tone 1954 Ford sedan. There was the 'purple cow' station wagon, which I have no idea what make, model or year it was. Another was a red 1957 Chevrolet four-door, a 1937 Ford sedan, and a two-door black 1956 Chevy, or the guy's 1950 Studebaker that we all rode in to Cordova. We cruised Cedar Rapids. It was twenty-five cents or less for a gallon of gas. Henry's Hamburgers out on 16th Avenue S.W. next to Shady Acres Motel was a one-stop store. Fifteen-cent hamburgers and cheeseburgers sold for 20 cents. The A&W on Ellis Blvd. N.W. (which is still there) and a must stop was Park Lane Drive-In at 1971 16th Ave. S.W. also out on 16th Avenue. Driving down Ellis Blvd. towards the park on a Saturday afternoon was like driving down the street of some sort of worldly renowned Hollywood, Miami Beach or Acapulco vacation spot. The river on our right and the swimming pool coming up next was when we entered the 'cool zone," Ellis Park itself. That park is still a beautiful place where everybody who was anybody hung out. One would even notice some strangers who were possibly east side guys standing around with their exotic and rich-looking east side girlfriends. There was a pizza restaurant on First Avenue West that we used to bounce Washington guys out of a couple of times each year. Our attitudes were, 'How dare they wear their red and white leather-sleeved school jackets on the west side.' We usually made it a point to stop at the EastSide Maid-Rite with our Jefferson blue and white jackets occasionally to show off the 'colors.' No one patrolled Cedar Rapids in those days like we did. We kept everything in order—or at least we thought we did. I still don't know why it was so important to keep things separated. Sometimes we'd get way out there around Washington High School. In one instance, someone had splattered red paint and left graffiti all over the main portico entrance to Jefferson High School. We got together and promptly did the very exact thing to Washington's main entrance with blue paint. However, our graffiti was a bit more graphic. We would even go way out into Marion and get our clocks cleaned. Too far into the breach—maybe we won't patrol out so far next time—we decided to stay a little closer to home.

One time, maybe after a homecoming or other football game, Jefferson students drove around the west side in a large multi-car caravan. The front cars decided to stop in the middle of the Third Avenue bridge and cause a huge traffic jam for people heading to the east side. Everybody just stopped everything from moving. The stopped cars then decided to lift the hoods of their cars. After a while, the police showed up with the three-wheeled motorcycles they used at that time and had to drive down the sidewalk to get to the lead cars. No reason to stop traffic, but when you're 16 or 17 years old, you don't think or realize the consequences of your actions.

We had created a huge mess and then continued on our merry way laughing at the prank we pulled. I don't recall any citations being issued either.

I had a 1954 Ford two-door. In the terminology of the time, it was "cherry." The ashtray had never been used. It had a V-8 engine and the entire automobile was clean, brand-new looking with not even a scratch or dent. The two-tone green bottom and cream top automobile took my friends and I about six months to completely trash. I first removed the stock hub caps and replaced them with baby moon hub caps. I then painted the rims black. I bought portawalls, the fake slim rubber white walls that were popular at the time. The car was slowly looking somewhat "cool," but not cool enough. We decided that it needed a manual transmission with a floor shift instead of an automatic transmission on the column. Automatic transmissions were for 'old people' and girls. We cut, chopped, tore out the floor board to add the gear shift and clutch assembly. The gear shift apparatus was a kit that could be purchased from the auto parts store. We took the stock muffler system out and replaced it with loud pipes. The air cleaner was removed and a small chrome pot was added. Cheap seat covers were then added and that completed the redo. I then finished it off by beating it to death with quick jack rabbit starts and smashing, grinding stops. Very seldom did I ever take it out of second gear, just so I could listen to the sound of my new, loud muffler system rumble when I left off the gas. Most teenagers still destroy their cars. The downtown loop, First Avenue, Second Avenue, and Third Avenue—then out to Sixteenth Avenue, Ellis Blvd., and Ellis Park. Round and round we went, over and over again—each taking a turn with one of our own cars. Four or five of us jammed into the car looking for girls, honking and saluting fellow cruisers, stopping at all the hot spots. In my years of cruising, I don't ever recall picking up any females or even having them acknowledge us and wave back for that matter, not even from Jefferson unless we already knew them. We never gave up the search—we went far and wide.

A couple of times, we rode horses from Upmeyers Stables. Of course, the quarry at Fairfax and the Amana Colonies to see what was going on down there. We would visit two girls who were sisters in Lisbon, and the short road trips to Palisades-Kepler State Park. Palisades was pretty and somewhat secluded. You could go way back there and park your car, find a lake shore and have a party. One summer evening, after returning to a nice spot we discovered earlier that week, a group of us were having some cocktails and snacks with our girlfriends. Ten or 12 of us were on a pleasant sandy beach area. We were well into the party and sitting around our small campfire when a park ranger stopped along the rutted road above and behind us. He then shone his spotlight down upon our gathering. He told us the park was closing and that we needed to extinguish the fire. He also said, "I hope you kids aren't drinking anything with alcohol down there." The girls, as I mentioned before, were way ahead of us and had already began covering up and burying the Sloegin, lime-flavored vodka and beers there on the beach. By the time the park ranger arrived with his flashlight, everything had magically disappeared. He did a quick scan around the area with his flashlight and waited for us until the fire was properly put out. On our way home, we devised a plan to return to the site the following day to retrieve our buried treasure. The next day we went back to the spot on the beach in the afternoon and began digging. We dug, and then dug some more.

"Where the heck was that stuff?"

"Right here…I know it." So we dug some more.

"Where is it? It has to be right here!" We dug up an area about 50 feet square. There were holes everywhere…nothing.

"That park ranger must have come back and got it," someone mused.

"Oh, that bastard!" We were in shocked disbelief at the treachery.

We drug our shovels back up to the car and threw them into the trunk in utter disgust.

"Man, you can't trust anybody anymore."

We returned to Cedar Rapids in the evening and went home empty-handed. By the next evening, the girls had called and told us that it was going to be women's night out that evening and that we were free to do whatever. They wouldn't tell us where they were going or what they were up to. At first, we thought it to be a little suspicious, but then forgot about it. Well, the girls had beat us to the stash at the beach and decided to have their own private party at one of their houses. They kept all the empty bottles and showed them off to us, laughing and teasing, "Neener, neener…" They laughed even louder when they repeated and mimicked our whiney voices explaining how much earth we had moved searching to no avail because of the supposed park ranger thief. It was a great joke. We had two or three good woodsie's out there at Palisades during our high school days.

Drag racing our cars wasn't a big part of our activities or daily life during the summer. However, there was a quarter-mile strip marked off south of town on 'J' Street, I believe, way out towards Prairie Creek that we used a few times. We also raced from stoplight to stoplight in town now and then. Nobody had the fast, souped up automobile. Most of the guys I hung out with were pretty responsible or too chicken to take the chance of an accident or worse, get a ticket. None of us made a lot of money either to afford fast engines. I did manage to blow up my mom's 1958 Oldsmobile on the way out to Palisades one night. I think my Ford was still in my friend's father's shop getting fitted with the new manual transmission. What a screw up I was. My father had died in an accident a little over a year earlier and now I ruined my mother's car. It was towed to a repair shop in Cedar Rapids and the engine was replaced. My job was only to destroy things while in high school. That is probably one of the reasons I gave my own son wide parameters and not much trouble when he would mess up. Everyone screws up a few times. It's when it becomes a habit that you'll know something is wrong.

One of the guys I knew had the coolest cruise mobile—a 1937 Ford sedan with a flat-head motor and it wasn't in bad condition. He somehow managed to overturn it out on 1st Avenue East one evening while steering with his bare feet. We sat along the curb waiting for the cops or someone to stop. Nobody came, so we pushed it back upright and drove off. There was another time in the old Ford at Ellis Park when one day we came flying down a hill from somewhere in the park onto Ellis Road. It was too much of an angle for the old car, and he lost control and we started to roll over. His driver's side door suddenly swung open and got caught on the pavement stopping the car from rolling into the river. It was stupid luck.

Sometimes we would go hunting north of town in the Old Classic. I had a 4-10 shotgun that was a single shot. The barrel broke down and you had to insert one shell into it, then snap it all back into place. You then needed to move the safety switch to off and you were ready to shoot. We would walk through the woods and shoot at almost anything that moved. We hunted for rabbits while walking along the railroad tracks and pheasants in the corn rows in November. When pheasants fluttered and warbled up from the stalks, my first and only shot would kick up the dirt 10 feet in front of me. The two guys I was hunting with one day both shot a squirrel each. We made a fire in the woods, gutted and skinned the squirrels, then stuck their carcasses on a stick like marshmallows and cooked them over the open flame. We ate both of the squirrels right there. I don't think any of us had actual training with guns and had no idea how we ever kept from shooting each other. I think it was good that we only went hunting a few times during our junior and senior years in high school.

"Mexicans? What Mexicans?" someone said.

"You know, what's his name from Washington, and his brother."

Apparently, one of the two brothers from Washington had moved in on our friend's girlfriend and was explaining his problem to us. Well, gee whiz, we can't have that going on.

After finding out exactly who the perpetrators were, we paused a minute to contemplate. It was okay to hassle some goofy bookworm from the east side, but these two guys were different.

"Where did you say they lived, up behind the Y?"

Our friend must have been crazy to think we'd go up there and start trouble. You just didn't know what would happen. We quickly forgot about any retaliation, but a while later, it started up again. This time it began with a confrontation and threats to both our friend and his girlfriend. All right, here we go, not even knowing or caring about hearing both sides of the story. The hunt was on. While heading east on 1st Avenue, an unbelievable thing happened. We spotted both guys driving directly ahead of us. There were five of us and we wheeled up beside them hurling insults and threats at them out of our window from the safety of our car. They tried to lose us, but we kept up at every sharp turn and evasive maneuver they made. They finally cut and headed straight for home. No problem for us, we had their address. Well, according to our friend, at least the correct house. We went behind the Y.M.C.A. building slowly driving up Fifth Street to 'A' Avenue, 'B' Avenue, and then 'C' Avenue. We went down to Fifth, back around again, driving all over back there very slowly and starting to get confused. We began noticing a lot of guys and girls just hanging around their parked cars, porch steps and sidewalks as they watched us cruise around the neighborhood like tin ducks at an arcade. I think our slow moves at finding the correct house, combined with the disappearance of the two brothers we were chasing, gave our quarry time to mobilize the troops, so to speak. We weren't familiar with the area, and after a couple of wrong turns, we began to get nervous.

"Why don't we just take off for now and come back another time?" asked the driver. There was an anxious chorus of, "Yeah, okay, good idea."

Just then, car headlights appeared behind us, drove up swiftly and then bumped the rear bumper of our car and then backed off a few feet—not gently either. I thought, 'How rude.' We stopped—they stopped. We got out of the car, they got out of the car. We took one look at these guys and it was like a bunch of circus clowns all trying to pile back into our 'miniature clown mobile' all at once.

"Go, go, go!" Our car shot off leaving some of us running alongside desperately trying to dive through the window of the moving vehicle.

"Stop, stop, stop!" The car then came to an abrupt stop, slamming people into the opened doors.

"Go, go, go!" Off we flew again, everyone safely abroad.

The guys must have had a good long laugh, because it took a while for them to catch up with us. They were angry and big. I've never seen a meaner group of guys in my life, and now they were gaining ground on us. They weren't using proper driving etiquette either, and that disturbed us. They were all over the place, with apparent malice on their minds. Down a street at one point in front of a church and back again, we were lost and couldn't find 1st Avenue. It had momentarily vanished, and panic began to set in.

"Turn here, no…turn there!" Everybody was talking at once and there didn't seem to be any street lights.

Finally, we magically appeared, crossing 1ˢᵗ Avenue and then it was all out flight homeward bound. The car that was chasing us turned off with hoots, hollers and shaking fists. We beat it back across the river safely and had a good laugh on ourselves over the sheer terror we had experienced when things had backfired and turned on us. It wasn't pretty at all, our 'little Mexico fiasco.'

Now, when did the Mexican Americans first begin to appear in Cedar Rapids? Well, myself, of course, had never heard Spanish being spoken or hearing anything from family or friends concerning Hispanics in Cedar Rapids. In high school, it was the kid with the 1937 Ford sedan who was part of our group of friends and was one of us. There was no difference, you just didn't hear from, or about Hispanics or anything. Hispanics, like most people, were new to this area and were the silent minority. They slowly arrived, maintained and nurtured strong church activities, which sustained those first few families and kept everything going.

What was it that made the Hispanic people come to Iowa? It was the Mexican railroad workers that were hired by the Northern Railroad company who first came in 1916 through 1918. Most, if not all the families, actually lived in the box cars of the particular railroads the men worked for. These people were very poor, probably poorer and with less money than any of our other immigrants or new arrivals. Many of the first Mexican-American families literally lived from hand to mouth. They struggled, survived, and during the second World War, they sent their sons into the military to protect America. Another influx from the southwest part of the United States arrived during the war period under a government program that allowed Mexican Nationals to come to the United States to work on the railroads and factories to help fill the wartime manpower shortage. My own father worked for the Milwaukee Road at the time also and was exempt from military duty. That's how important railroad jobs were. After the war, more arrived, including other family members and friends of those that were already in Cedar Rapids.

During the 1960's, a number of Mexican-American families moved up from Texas to Cedar Rapids as migrant workers. They found permanent jobs here after a while and decided to stay. In 1973, an organization was formed called, 'Los Amigos' to try and keep the Mexican-American tradition and social activities going in this area. Although families of Mexican-American or Hispanic heritage were dispersed into all parts and neighborhoods of Cedar Rapids, a heavy concentration of people could be found behind the old Y.M.C.A. on 1st Avenue and 5th Street N.E. Today, the neighborhood is mostly gone because of Interstate 380. The Interstate going through the city is a good thing, but it did take away from all those old environments I had grown up and experienced life in.

Danceland ballroom was downtown on 'A' Avenue and 3rd Street N.E., 'Iowa's Smartest Ballroom' was opened in 1927 and the big bands of that era played there. A walk up a flight of stairs took you into wonderland. There was a bowling alley on the ground floor and when I was 16 or so, a buddy of mine and I went down to Danceland one evening. It was my first time. He was resolute about going down there, so I said, "Okay, why not?" I didn't even know what Danceland was all about or even exactly where it was located. When we arrived and entered the bowling alley below, he brought me over to a row of enclosed phone booths in the back, picked up the telephone in one particular booth and pressed his ear against the receiver. A smile fell across his face, and a moment later, he handed me the phone.

"Listen just a minute and you can hear the band playing upstairs."

Oh man, I thought. For some strange dynamized reason, one could actually hear a band rocking out upstairs over the receiver.

"Can you hear it, can you?" he said, snatching the phone back to his ear to listen to more. His head was bobbing up and down to the beat of the electronic crackle.

"How in the heck did you figure this out?" I asked. Thinking this is one whacked out musical affeciondo. He never answered.

"Wanna sneak in?" he said. "Ah, not really," I replied. But it was a popular group at the time. I still remember it was the Hollywood Argyles singing their hit song, 'Alley oop,' when we just walked up the carpeted ascent and entered Danceland. The smell of alcohol wafted over us. No one was at the door because it was the Argyles' last song of the night and the doorman didn't care anymore. The show was over, but it was my first vision of a popular recording group performing on stage.

I strolled around the place with my friend awhile, feeling very uncomfortable. I then stepped back down the stairs with some of the patrons who were leaving. That was my first introduction to Danceland Ballroom. It wasn't my last. I couldn't recall how the place caught on with us after my initial contact. I was probably listening to radio advertisements by the promoters that brought the popular bands that entertained at Danceland or from word of mouth. We waited each week to see who would be there on the weekend. Danceland sold beer through a small window located on the right side of the stage. You had to show your ID for every purchase. There was the stage, which was three, or four feet above the dance floor that was lined on both sides with round cabaret-style tables and chairs. The likes of Leslie Gore, Joey Dee and the Starlighters, Everly Brothers, the Beach Boys and Jerry Lee Lewis, to name a few, came to perform.

There was a cover charge at the entrance and then they stamped the back of your hand with something fluorescent when placed under an ultraviolet light. The purpose of this was so that you could leave during intermission and come back in later. I was impressed with the Big City, adult technology. It didn't take long for someone to come up with a fake ID. Iowa's driver's license was light green with the information typewritten in by hand. No pictures, thumb prints or anything else. What made our fake driver's license unique was that it wasn't an Iowa license, but one from Utah, and it was a real one. The problem, though, was the date of birth showed the bearer to be 23. None of us even looked 16. We also found out that only one beer could be served to one person at a time and not five or six like we had anticipated. We finally found someone who bravely walked up to the window, lay down the driver's license from Utah and purchase a single beer. He promptly strutted back to our table with his trophy, sat down and we all took a couple of sips. When the bottle was empty, he walked back to the window again but became befuddled when the lady started to question him about Salt Lake City and also asked to see a draft card or something else with his name on it. He returned empty and that was the end of our alcohol buying, fake identification program. It was good for one beer only. Soft drinks were alright, but we were manly men and since we wouldn't be able to consume alcohol at Danceland, we would consume it outside during the band breaks. Across the street in an alley was the spot we picked. There was a parking space halfway down for automobiles with a short wooden railing along the side with enough room for a couple of cars. All we needed to do was have someone buy us a case of beer, ice it down, place it in the trunk of one of the cars, and there, it would be waiting for us whenever we wanted. Absolutely brilliant. We were the smartest guys in town. The very first Saturday night we implemented our plan, everything went well. Out for a couple of beers, back into Danceland. Back out again, cross the street, open the trunk get some more beers out and sit along the fence. It was splendid in its simplicity. When the police car whipped into the alley and skidded to a stop in front of us, we all sat stunned an instant, then beers flew in the air and we scattered helter skelter in every direction back to Danceland. Up the stairs we panted in small groups, showed our remarkable invisible stamp to the doorman and disappeared inside and underneath a table of lady friends. In the early 1960's, girls wore dresses with things called petty coats underneath. Sometimes two or three of them at a time to extend or blossom out the outside skirt. So when you have a group of women wearing those things, they cover anything going on under a table. We peaked out from between the skirts to see policemen walking around inside looking for us. The police were committed back then. Gum chewing in school, truancy, and smoking cigarettes were bad, but underage alcohol consumption on city streets and in alley ways were frowned upon a bit more, and these police officers were dedicated. They looked everywhere, even walking right past our table. They finally gave up the search of Danceland and left. We slowly re-emerged one by one from under the table again ending our well laid plans.

After the Cedar River flooded in 1961, the City of Cedar Rapids paid a tribute to the citizens of the city for coming together in a time of need and help during the crisis. They called it the 'Sandbaggers Hop' and held a big party and dance at Danceland Ballroom that summer. The place was torn down in 1973 to make room for the new Five Seasons Center.

When I first entered high school at Jefferson, we were all introduced to the American Field Service for the first time. I had heard something about it before. It's where American kids traveled to a foreign country and lived with a host family during the course of the school year. These host families also had a child who went to the same school along with the visiting kid. Boys stayed with a family with a boy and the girl stayed with the girls. It was exactly the same for students who stayed with American families. Laos, Germany, Turkey, Spain, Japan and Portugal were the countries involved whose children stayed with families in Cedar Rapids and attended Jefferson. These foreign exchange students were definitely different from our Midwestern ways. It was odd for most of us to understand or even try to comprehend them. There was a girl from Turkey who was quite pretty and would get long lingering glances as she walked down the halls to her class. However, she didn't want to have anything to do with us, which made her enticing. There were no double dates or coed group events away from school, nothing much to our displeasure. There was a guy from Portugal and that was a different story. It took a while for him to be noticed. In the interest of international brotherhood and understanding, we decided to include him in our little click. He said that when he arrived in town, he had come with only two suitcases—one for clothing and the other filled with bottles of Portuguese wine. He became our new instant friend, and it wasn't an idle boast about the wine. He had the goods. He was a real interesting fellow and enjoyed partying. He smiled a lot, was easy going, and was happy to be here. Once in a while, we would stop by his house and pick him up so he could cruise around with us, even after we had drank all his wine. He offered a different view on things and it was exotic hanging around with someone from Portugal.

My mother, stepfather, two brothers and my sister left for vacation in the summer of 1963. They filled the station wagon up to the roof with stuff for the trip.

Mt. Rushmore, Rocky Mountain National Park, and the Grand Canyon was their destination. They were on their way to travel the entire western part of the United States and would be gone for a few weeks. They left me in charge of the house. I was given explicit instructions on how to maintain and care for our home in their absence. I was given the keys to the house with complete and utter trust. The first few days went pretty well. I just worked my part-time job and hung around the house and had a few friends over.

I worked down in the basement of the Sun Mart Town & Country Center on First Avenue East with another kid from Jefferson. He's the one who got me the job. We silk-screened window poster advertisements for a grocery store chain. It was artistic stuff, and since I was to attend art school in the fall, it was a great job to have. Our work included cutting out the outlines of each letter with an exacto knife on a film-like material. 'Such and such beans' three cans for $1.00 or 'Special-Cling Peaches 25 cents a can.' Promotional things like that. Then the film was etched or burned into the screen with a bright light. I've forgotten the exact silk screen process. The final etched screen was attached to a wood frame and laid over a blank piece of butcher-like paper. Ink was added and with a large squeegee, spread across the screen, transferring the cut-out words to the paper and then hung from a drying rack. The entire process was repeated over and over again. The advertisements in the windows of various supermarkets around town in 1963 were mostly likely manufactured by me and my friend. After a while, boredom set in, and we started doing our own personal posters.

After hurrying to finish our quotas, we would cut, print, and dry our own versions, and one of them consisted of a bright, colorful and psychedelic type background with the simple words, 'BEANIES BIRDLAND' imprinted in reverse print. My nickname in high school was 'The Bean' or 'Beanie.' 'Birdland' came from a verse of a popular song by Ray Charles. I must say, it was some terrific-looking graphic art. A bedroom wall wasn't good enough to hang this jewel. This piece of art had to be seen by the entire world. I brought it home and placed it in my mom's picture window. It covered the entire space. As the first week went by, more and more friends would stop by and hang out, adding to a group core who had almost moved in. We were sitting around one evening before heading out to patrol the west side, when we decided to have a party at 'Beanie's Birdland.' It was sort of a last-summer get together blast. Why not, I thought. My parents wouldn't return for at least two more weeks. Any mess that could result in such a party would be cleaned up like nothing had taken place. A few graduates from Jefferson and friends would attend, that's all. What could happen? The party had a slow start. I had some friends over in the later afternoon who helped set things up. Some of them left and returned later while others stayed and some arrived. Girls would stop by, leave, and then return. People casually had come and gone in the early evening, and I thought how boring the party had become. Oh well, we had a lot of beer on hand. Between 9 p.m. and 10 p.m., a number of people had shown up and stayed. It got busier and things were beginning to take off. Guys with dates who had graduated a year ahead of us showed up, guys with dates who were underclassmen—it was a hit, and I was the star. More and more people I had never known or seen before came. Where was everyone coming from, I wondered. I was having a great time and didn't really care. The kid from Portugal showed up with a bottle of wine in each hand and with him were a couple of foreign exchange students from Washington High. I didn't even know that he was still in the country. A childhood friend from my Linwood Cemetery days came in with a ton of east side people. The party was becoming out of control. People from Vinton, Lincoln Way Village, Marion and Mechanicsville were also attending this party. How did everyone find out about the party? The Deborah Drive area around my house was blocked with parked cars, and there were a lot of cars in the driveway and front lawn area. I surveyed the house and got nervous. A person had difficulty negotiating through the rooms of the house because they were jam packed. Every room was occupied. The downstairs linoleum basement floor had one-eighth to one-quarter of an inch of beer sloshing around from the kegs of beer we all chipped in to purchase. The basement was also packed with inebriated teenagers and young adults standing wall to wall with music blaring in the background. I then realized that I had lost all authority and had become a stranger in my own home. It was difficult to describe this event, as I was amazed at the masses of people. I found my way out and even saw people in the garage, standing amongst the parked cars in the driveway, front lawn and street. As I re-entered the house, something caught my eye coming from the back yard. As I went to investigate, I found the entire yard lighted up with blinking yellow road sign lights. There appeared to be hundreds of them. Someone had obviously taken them from road construction sites and placed them in my back yard. They were like gigantic, monstrous fireflies, all twinkling crazily on and off. What was really incomprehensible was that the police department never showed up. I decided to forget everything and deal with it later the next day. Around 3 a.m. in the morning, I toured the house looking at the carnage. Mostly everyone had gone—yet there were some people here and there. I crawled off somewhere and fell asleep. The next morning I awoke to a couple of friends dragging me up to my feet.

"Bean, get up. We have to do something!"

The first thing I noticed was that my mom's beige carpet had black trails where the foot traffic was the heaviest—black. There were cases of empty beers stacked almost to the ceiling. Someone had taken the time, before I awoke, to go around the house and pick up all the empties and place them back into the empty cases.

"Wow, what a party," someone blurted. I walked around in a daze, with my girlfriend helping me along the way.

"Don't worry, we'll all pitch in and get this mess cleaned up," she said. It seemed most of my friends had split when things started getting out of control. They returned to help me pick up the pieces. Nothing was actually broken, just soiled and dirty. We actually started to get things back into some semblance of order, although we started drinking again—not heavy, just a couple of beers while we straightened things up. Everyone was fabulous, especially our girlfriends. We opened all the doors and windows and picked up the trash. A neighbor drove by with his wife and slowed down. Oh, oh, I thought, trying to ignore what would be coming up next.

"Hey," my neighbor yelled out of his car window. "Beanie's Birdland!" Oh man, were they here too? By 7 p.m., we had almost gotten things straightened out when a car load of guys showed up and asked, "Is this where the party's at?"

"That was last night you morons!" someone remarked back, tired from the day's cleaning up. They continued to drive on. That was an ominous sign for me for some reason. By 10 p.m. that night, my house had transformed itself. Slowly and subtly, it became once again, the place to be. I succumbed once again, when, down in the basement, a group of guys were sitting on the sofa toasting Jefferson wrestlers. When they all threw their heads back to imbibe, they flew backwards over the sofa. Their arms and legs flailing and beer went everywhere. The next morning the yellow road sign lights were still blinking in the back yard and the house was almost in the same shape it was before. Not too many unknown people sleeping things off this time.

"Okay, this is it," I said in a final show of disgust. I still had a few days before my family would come home from their vacation. There was a lot of time to straighten things out. No police were involved yet. I was serious and had a lot to do as I slopped around the basement. My mother had told me not to use the washing machine because it was broken. Our girlfriends had tried to help by doing all the laundry and bedding in the house. A large mess ensued; but no problem, this can all be resolved. I just needed time. The following day, everyone of my friends pulled together and pitched in to help. They mopped the basement floor, yet it was still a little sticky. We had a carpet cleaner ready to rent and was going to take all the wet, greasy marked laundry to a Laundromat. All the blinking yellow road signs had been removed from the back yard. We left our work to go and get something to eat for lunch at a fast-food place and left the girls behind to continue with the cleaning. We would then take a lunch break. While we were all packed in a 1960 Blue Ford convertible eating lunch, my family had pulled up behind us. In writing this, I had just become a bit upset and am unable to continue on except to say—they came home early. By the way, a week before I left for Colorado, I wrecked the front end of my mom's Oldsmobile gain. I left for art school, but in my mind, I felt like a failure and very dismal.

As we already know, 1673 is the year first recorded for European visitors to this area. Marquette and Jolliet, in 1690, Nicolas Perrot built a trading post near Dubuque. The first influx were the French including Lasalle. In the early 1700's, a few fur traders and missionaries wondered around here, but didn't build any permanent settlements. In 1788, Julien Dubuque became the first permanent European settler in Iowa. By the early 1800's, Zebulon Pike surveyed the upper Mississippi, and this area became settled by people from the New England area. Also, immigrants new to America came from Northern and Central Europe. More and more of them came from the eastern and southern states. Some stayed and some moved on. In the 1840's a second major wave of immigration had begun. Irish, English, German, Dutch, Czechoslovakian and Scandinavian immigrants came from all over Europe. Cedar Rapids was founded and settled by these people. A lot with German ancestry. A few generations later, most traditions and customers of their country were eventually forgotten. Today, less than 2% of the people in Iowa are foreign born. Germans are still the majority in Iowa.

I have learned that the traditions and things faded away as time went on. The newer generation just don't seem to care anymore about the old ways because they are living in a brand new environment. There are new ways of celebrating this or that—new made-up ways and customs to fit the local peoples' land and harvest. Everyone kind of forgets the old traditional ways, and besides, the European heritage is vast and ancient. It would be impossible to retain everything. Every day would be a holiday in some form or another. People adapt to the new way things are done. There are, of course, resurges of ethnic culture now and then to remember ancestors and customs from the old country; however, even then some of them are forgotten because of lack of interest. They retained or we retained only the ones all people could enjoy. For example, October fest, Cinco De Mayo, St. Patrick's Day, Chinese New Year, Columbus Day, Thanksgiving, etc. All of these celebrations are derived from the old world but suited and shaped to fit into our own American culture.

It was the Europeans who first recorded finding this place and the Europeans who founded it. All those who followed added the sugar and spice, the glue that made it strong. There were numerous bridges built over the Cedar River, but the only one that stayed intact and managed to stay erect was a bridge at 7th Avenue that was built in 1856. A toll bridge on 1st Avenue was built in 1859. These were the ones that helped continue Cedar Rapids onto what it is today. The Red Cedar River and the bridges over it is why Cedar Rapids is a city. The swift current of the cedar made grain milling a natural. The railroad which was another must came in 1859. These important few things are why Cedar Rapids flourished in the early days. Fertile land to farm, having water and transportation was all you needed for more people to follow. The City of Cedar Rapids grew and expanded along the east side of the river. When the railroad came, the rails slowed traffic eastward. A viaduct was built over the railway to accommodate traffic and pedestrians to travel and expand the city. More buildings, parks, businesses and residential areas appeared. Grain, cereal and corn syrup were the base products. That is what made the city. The Europeans, Hispanics, Blacks, and Arabs all contributed to the growth and production of the city. It took many people together to help make Cedar Rapids what it is today. People from outside the Midwest more than likely considered this Red Neck Central. Did you know that Cedar Rapids has the highest college educated people per capita? It's quiet along the Cedar, like a sanctuary. All you had to do to maintain the status quo was to assure a future and the right to earn a buck. Is there discourse and disunity? Of course, but has it boiled over into big time destruction or injury?

Sinclair Meat Packing opened in town in 1871, the first telephone was installed in 1877. There were major advancements going on. There were gas streetlamps in 1871 and the Wright Brothers, Orville and Wilbur lived in Cedar Rapids and attended elementary school.

The first electric lights were displayed in Cedar Rapids during a Barnum and Bailey's Circus in 1881. Imagine what a spectacle that must have been. I wish I could have been there. It's hard to envision what the parents and children experienced at that time.

"Daddy, Daddy, what is that?" Not a single glowing bulb, but an entire canvas tent was filled with glowing orbs. One hundred and twenty years later, I can feel the effect of that scene on the people who witnessed the panorama and pageant that was laid before them, not to mention the circus that was going on at the same time. It was definitely worth a quarter. During my Linwood Cemetery days, my friends and I came across the headstone and grave of the Cherry Sisters. It was in the older part of Linwood at the edge of an old road leading to the cemetery entrance from 'L' Street. I mentioned the old headstone and the sisters' name to my mom. She informed me that they were famous singers and entertainers in the Cedar Rapids area during the late 1890's and early 1900's.

In 1905, a terrible fire destroyed the Quaker Oats plant. This, after many years of building growth for Cedar Rapids, was rebuilt within a year. The Douglas Starch Works across the river exploded in 1919 and there was loss of life; however, the city continued on with rebuilding and even building an airplane landing field that same year.

In 1928, the Veteran's Memorial Building and Coliseum was built on May's Island. May's Island is also an integral part of Cedar Rapids. It is the heart of the city and one of the things that make it unique is that it was named for a former owner of the island by the name of Colonel John M. May. 1936 was a great year for Cedar Rapids as far as I was concerned. The first 'All Iowa Fair' was held there. I used to go with my folks and siblings when I was a child. I couldn't get enough of that cotton candy. The smells and sounds of the dusty Midway, the clunking and creaking of the rides, carnival workers shouting at passers by, "Win a Kewpie Doll for your lady," were the things any child would enjoy. There was the Hawkeye Downs Midget Racing. When I was in high school, there were girls from all over surrounding counties visiting the fair. We used to drive past Prairie Creek, park our cars, walk back along the railroad tracks, probing the fairs outer fringes for a way to sneak in. It worked a few times until the fair grounds posted police all along the back side. It was easier to just pay the admission and park your car in the lot. One evening, we got together with some other Jefferson students. Four of us got separated from the main group—three guys and a girl. We decided that we were going to see a 'freak show.' There were a couple of shows at the fair. There was one particular show that featured a real life hermorphadite. I didn't quite know what a hermorphadite was, but I knew it had something to do with the sexuality of a person. We entered the show area and the girl led the way and we followed behind, and I was not sure what we were getting ourselves into. You would pay the initial price to see the show and then if you wanted, you could pay a little more to see the 'next show.' That show was more risqué and after it ended, there were six or seven people still sitting on wooden picnic benches, including us, waiting for the finale. The finale costs more and we were told it would be worth the extra money to be able to witness 'one of God's amazing aberrations,' right here and right now in the flesh. The emcee made everyone all swear, in a hushed tone, we were not undercover police before he opened the flap of a tent that went even deeper into the inner sanctum. He motioned to us to enter and gather around. We did so in silence; then a curtain opened, and there, reclining before us, was possibly the most obese human being I had ever seen. He or she wore a robe, and it was quite bizarre. We got our money's worth. This person disrobed and laid back exposing a penis through many folds of fat. My head jerked back, eyes transfixed. Alright, that's enough. The girl that was with us grabbed my arm and said, "Wait, wait a minute." As she leaned in and surveyed the person posing, I stepped back completely embarrassed with the entire situation. I glanced at my buddy and his eyes were wide open. His head was moving slowly back and forth in disbelief. It was the talk of the town among us for a couple of weeks after that. I was sorry I spent the money, but hey, it was the 'All Iowa Fair.'

By 1937, Cedar Rapids had the new police station built and in 1944 the first municipal airport was ready for airplanes. A full-fledged city arose, and now Cedar Rapids has everything in place—a municipality ready for modern commerce. The river was always there for us. It milled our grain and now gave us electricity. The Butterfly Café, Bishop's Cafeteria, and The Flame Room, The Dragon, Kozy Inn and Danceland Ballroom were places in Cedar Rapids that are now gone but not forgotten.

COLOR OF THE RIVER

CHAPTER FIVE

CHAPTER FIVE

Cedar Rapids, Iowa recognized a small building boom in the 1970's. River Front Park Downtown, Interstate 380 was opened and Cedar River Tower was an apartment building right on the river. Five Seasons Civic Center and Westdale Mall was also built in the 1970's. It was also in the 1970's when a new and different crew arrived in town. The Asians. My wife's first name is Thêhà. It's phonetically pronounced Tay-ha, and it literally means, 'Color of the River,' an appropriate name for stories that explain Cedar Rapids' ethnic diversities. Thêhà is Vietnamese and came from a country that originated 2,500 years ago. This ethnic group of people called the Viet emigrated south from the coastal area of China. Vietnam means *Verbatim*, the people (Viet) of the south (Nam). Asian folk, especially Vietnamese, began to appear on the scene in Cedar

Rapids in the early 1970's. Just a trickle at first, mostly the wives of U.S. servicemen who had served in Southeast Asia and Vietnam, or in a few cases, individuals who were helped out of trouble by civilians under contract in the area at the time and who wanted to get out. By 1980, a larger influx of Vietnamese arrived in the U.S. Included were some of the relatives of Vietnamese wives. We've all heard the term 'boat people' but not of the people who struggled and sacrificed their lives to get to the United States or anywhere safe for that matter. These people left due to the unfair and strict government. Not only did Thêhà and her family feel the hostile effects, but also the countless other South Vietnamese families as well. The Vietnamese people that arrived in America, raised their children, put them in school, learned English, stayed married, got divorced, got driver's licenses, started businesses, remarried or moved to other parts of the United States. Small island-like families stayed around Cedar Rapids who were in some way, in a form of cultural shock. They still managed to function—looking in wonderment at the first snowfall. As with all new immigrants, work ethics took over. If they couldn't understand English, they learned it. If they had no money, they worked to earn it. If they needed to earn more, they went to college, found a beneficiary, and looked for a City, State or Federal grant or endowment. They took advantage of anything that was available to those of refugee status. With the assistance of interdenominational church organizations, whole families and individuals were sponsored while waiting in refugee camps. These people were ready to go anywhere—France, Australia,

Canada, or the United States. It didn't matter because they couldn't go home. Why not Cedar Rapids, Iowa? I think I have a cousin there. Where is it? Army of the Republic of Vietnam (ARVN) military veterans were dealt with cruelly after the fall of Saigon. ARVN military officers to the level of Lieutenant were forced into re-education camps for five years and then after completion, five or more years were spent in prison. No work was made available to them afterwards either. Got to leave.

More Vietnamese started to emerge and spring up on census counts. As the initial group got larger, the Vietnamese people began to sponsor their family members waiting in camps that were located in the Philippines, Guam, and other holding areas in greater South East Asia. Thêhà, herself, was in the Philippines for a number of months before a Catholic Charities organization sponsored her to come to the United States. It helped a lot that she could already read, write and speak English and had someone already in California who could help her. She immediately found a job. Most of the other sponsored people and families couldn't speak any English or have any relatives that could help them. These people endured and adapted to their new life in Cedar Rapids after going through minus twenty degree-temperatures with snow and nothing familiar for them to relate to. They dealt with it just like everyone already living in Cedar Rapids.

The Vietnamese Friendship Association was led by a group in the mid 1980's to help arriving refugees and to consolidate the approximately 30 or 40 families already living in Cedar Rapids with their own customs and culture, with the, 'Don't Forget Your Heritage' concept. This organization slowly folded in the Cedar Rapids area. The young Asian Americans have become too Americanized to the sad dismay of older folk who sacrificed and strived to make a better life for their families. The younger generation were not interested—too busy raising their families and trying to make ends meet. Every one of us know that certain things manifest themselves when raising a family and striving towards that illusive American dream. There are 500 to 600 Vietnamese Americans living in the Cedar Rapids area along with 2,000 or so others of Asian descent. This is a minority group.

A cohesive organization that forwards Vietnamese heritage and language should be more widely accepted among the Vietnamese living here, I would say. The local Vietnamese community has its anti-communist group, as in Southern California, which is probably the country's largest. These groups are divided with those who want their country back some time in the future and those who have resigned themselves in the knowledge that nothing can be done and it's over. I know how important it is for Thêhà to speak with her family on the telephone occasionally. We visit them when we can. She misses Vietnam terribly and prays to Buddha twice a day without fail at her small shrine in our home. She applies her Vietnamese-style cuisine when she cooks our meals and sometimes she cries openly over her brothers who were killed in defense of South Vietnam. She laments over the loss of her country bitterly.

New people are an integral part of this city. They keep it progressive and vibrant. Immigrants and new people arrive from all over the world which will make Cedar Rapids a diverse and more interesting place to live.

Cedar Rapids progressed more so in the 1980's with a ground transportation center on 1st Street S.E. between 4th and 5th Avenue among other things and also a new Cedar Rapids Public Library. Growth and renewal occurred over time, but the 1990's didn't bode well for us. We lost around an estimated 2,000 people in the 1990 census. When other cities were experiencing increased surges in employment and population, we actually were losing people during the Dot Com bubble. Cedar Rapids remained solid and rebounded with 12,000 new citizens in the year 2000. There are cities and states that aren't doing well now. Even Cedar Rapids is experiencing a down turn. I can see from afar that the politics of Cedar Rapids will keep the city continuing slowly forward, even through tough economic times while other cities with no one caring or guiding things along were growing in leaps and bounds. No one at the helm—just bigger and more. Need more tax base, then hand out more and more building and water permits. Who cares? Uncontrolled expansion causes more problems.

There is virtually no traffic problems here in Cedar Rapids. The rest of the planet is a quagmire of automobiles—the founding progression of Cedar Rapids—a tough row to hoe? Basically yes, but we seemed to plod along and slowly travel forward. Now look at what our forefathers gave us—a wonderful city.

Is Cedar Rapids clean and neat? As good as most places. Does the garbage get picked up; do the roads and streets stay repaired? Does the snow get removed from the major arterials? I've lived in and seen cities where these basic things are pretty lax. Storm drainage, sewer systems and pure water from the tap. EMS, police and firefighters—they are all here to take care of business, and as far as I'm concerned, beyond professional about it. They care, I know this first hand. I realize most of these things are normal things that cities have to address. If it didn't snow here, it would be a sort of paradise with a river flowing through it. Well, okay, perhaps I'm a bit exuberant. I personally hated having to scrape an eighth of an inch of ice off my windshield at 7 a.m. with five degree below zero temperatures and scraping it with a cheap plastic scraper I got from some promotion somewhere that snaps in half after a couple of strokes, and that's when it seems really stupid to live here. Why do we put up with this? How and why did they do it before us? The Europeans, Afro-Americans, Asians, Arabians, Hispanics, and Native Americans that make up this city. We've got history, the entire spectrum is here. Every continent in the world is involved. I wonder, sometimes, what the first people were thinking. Why here? Well, because of the fertile land and accessibility. There was a river, the river no one notices anymore as we drive over the bridge.

Cedar Rapids has one of the finest public school systems in America with higher education available at Kirkwood Community College, a public two-year school offering Associate Degrees with over 11,500 students. Mount Mercy College a private four-year college, offers Bachelor's and Master's Degrees and having almost 1,300 students. Hamilton College, another private four-year school offering Bachelor's and Associate Degrees. St. Luke's Hospital where I was born, has a Nursing and Post-Baccalaureate Degree. Anything you needed, as far as education goes is right here in Cedar Rapids. Agriculture, manufacturing and retail pretty much ruled around here as far as jobs went. However, high tech and communication-type work has recently made its presence known. A lot of people from outside are coming into Cedar Rapids. Case in point, in 1998, I came home for a class reunion and after late flights and mechanical problems with the airlines, I arrived in town around 2 a.m. I was standing outside with another guy who seemed to be in the same situation as I was. At 2 a.m., I was not going to call any of my family to come and pick me up at that hour. We both called various cab companies but were informed that cabs usually didn't run out to the airport after midnight because all flights had already arrived. That made sense, but after a while, a cab did show up. We stood there and looked apprehensively at each other.

"Want to share?" the guy asked me with an accent. The ride into town was interesting. It seemed he moved his entire family to Cedar Rapids from France to work at some new high tech company I had never heard of before. "Oh really?" I replied, surprised when he told me what he did—something to do with avionics that was definitely over my head. We pulled up in front of his house and it was huge. It was in some newly made neighborhood off Edgewood Road before the bridge. In the cab ride back over to my folk's house, I thought to myself, 'Somebody moved their entire family here from France to work in Cedar Rapids?' Another bit of shock came to me about a year later while I was in Hawaii. I was watching a documentary on a cable channel about airplane disasters. You know, how they happen and how the National Transportation Safety Board (NTSB) figures out exactly what went wrong. On this program, a team was down in the jungles of South America investigating a horrible crash involving an American-made aircraft. The hour-long proceedings focused on all aspects of the accident. While digging around the crash site, they finally found the 'black box' which was almost destroyed. Two NTSB investigators were talking back and forth with each other holding the 'black box.' A documentary camera filming away. After deciding the 'black box' was beyond hope that anything useful or important could be obtained from the unrecognizable, twisted metal, decided, matter-of-factly, "We're going to have to send this to Cedar Rapids. Somebody up there will figure it out."

Cedar Rapids stays under the radar. It is usually never mentioned on national news and when I'm asked where I was born, I say, "Cedar Rapids, Iowa." That reply is always met with a blank stare. "Where?" is the usual reply.

The more things I discover about Cedar Rapids, the more proud I am of it. There's only a core of professionals that know about this place. People living in Cedar Rapids are going to be able to take advantage of the area's high-tech opportunities that are going to be available if the city plays its cards right.

In 1933, Franklin Delano Roosevelt's new deal program that made the Civilian Conservation Corp and other public works building programs to give Americans employment opportunities during the depression era, with an emphasis on transportation and infrastructure for America. This treated Cedar Rapids well. Several young entrepreneurs emerged to develop companies that are still operating today. Paving the nation's roads played a big part in the success of this city's industry.

Howard Hall was an industrialist and philanthropist who founded Iowa Manufacturing. I remember it being located over on 16th Street N.E. by Daniel's Park. Mr. Hall had an ingenious machine that could crush stone into a ready-to-use base on site. His company revolutionized the road building industry. Iowa Manufacturing is now known as Cedar Rapids, Inc., an industry leader in producing equipment used for crushing, screening, asphalt mixing and paving. Also, in 1950, Mr. Hall and a small group of investors purchased a refrigeration plant in Amana, Iowa. Amana Appliances introduced the Radar Range. Better known as the microwave oven.

In 1931, a young man with a great interest in radio communication changed the course of Cedar Rapids' industry. His name was Arthur Collins. Collins' radio expanded into avionics in the 1960's which opened an entirely new arena of high technology communications and following equipment that went on to become a thriving division of Rockwell. Cedar Rapids has its roots in agriculture, but technological advancement, such as those coming from Rockwell, have revolutionized the process of farming with global positioning systems developed at the Cedar Rapids facility.

Today, Rockwell is the area's largest employer, providing thousands of jobs for engineers, high tech specialists, and more. The contributions made by Arthur Collins has had one of the most profound impacts on the history of this town. Furthermore, George Nissen's world famous Nissen Trampoline Company helped things along.

After surviving the Great Depression in the 1930's and prospering during the economic boom that followed the end of the World War II, the 1950's and 1960's were healthy times for the Cedar Rapids region. Prosperity was everywhere. Industry was growing. Our communities were growing. Infrastructure was being put in place for the future.

In the 1970's, several large equipment manufacturers with ties to farming, transportation and construction relocated, downsized and/or went out of business. We faced hard economic times and hard decisions in Cedar Rapids. Whatever caused this—is another story. However, in collaboration with Cedar Rapids area Chamber of Commerce, business leaders pooled financial resources and set in motion events that, today, may be seen as one of the country's most successful economic development projects. It was called 'Priority One.' I wrote the above and the following information from a web site concerning the Cedar Rapids Chamber of Commerce at www.cedarrapids.org/chamber/history, asp.

In the early 1980's, recognizing that a sound strategy for economic growth would be a start for development of the area, the Chamber of Commerce launched a full scale economic development program. The priority one plan was determined to bring many different types of new industry to the area. As a result, the labor force grew from 89,300 people in 1986 to 110,900 people in 1997. Unemployment fell from 7% in 1986 to 1.5% in 1998. Eighty-seven new companies opened facilities here, and nearly 200 existing businesses expanded providing our residents with a lot of quality jobs and security. Priority one projects have generated over $1.3 trillion in new taxable property.

Much of the Cedar Rapids area today mirrors our ancestry but with a modern high technology flare. From the Germans to the Czechs, we inherited a work ethic that is unmatched anywhere in the country. The blending of these first settlers and farmers with other immigrants from Scotland, Ireland and England created the diversity of culture that is the basis for our magnanimity and acceptance of all peoples. These words are exactly what this book is about.

A few years back, my brothers Larry and Mike walked into a restaurant bar one afternoon where Larry happened to notice a couple of friends sitting with another person. After introductions, we joined them. All of them were wearing flannel shirts with bib overalls and boots. They were a bunch of hard-working guys. During our conversation, I overheard one guy tell my brother, "Yeah, I hauled two loads this morning and another two already this afternoon." It seemed that everyone seated were truck drivers and all had made consecutive loads that day. The conversation began to change to something else when I blurted out,

"So, what do you guys haul?" The chitchat paused, and everyone looked at me momentarily, laughed, and then continued talking. Brother Larry leaned over towards me and simply stated, "Corn." How incredulously stupid of me, I thought. I mean, what else would anybody be hauling in Iowa? I laughed along with the group.

Farm machinery, of course, played a different, yet important part in the big picture around Cedar Rapids. From the time John Deere in 1837, came up with the self-polishing cast steel plow, to a man with the last name of Innes of Davenport, Iowa who, in 1936, invented an automatic bailer for hay. In 1842, a fellow by the name of Joseph Dart built the first grain elevator in and in 1850, Edmund Quincy invented the corn picker. With these basic inventions, things were going to change, and along with tractors, the entire agricultural industry was revolutionized. Corn makes the state of Iowa bloom.

I received the following information on the web at www.Cedar Rapids.org/chamber/history.asp.

Marion and Cedar Rapids have long shared boundaries, and today, it is difficult to tell when you cross from one community into another. Back in the frontier days, however, the boundaries were clear and the rivalry strong. Today, the rivalry is light-hearted and friendly, but there is still the question of why Marion Square's cannon is pointed in the direction of Cedar Rapids. In 1839, the site of the present town of Marion was chosen as the first Linn County seat. Residents of the newly formed town selected the name Marion as a tribute to the revolutionary war hero, General Francis 'Swamp

Fox' Marion. Through the 1920's, the railroad was the largest employer in Marion, with over 50% of the town's men employed by the industry. The railroad's influence helped shape Marion into a bustling commercial center that served both freight and passengers. Trains traveled directly through downtown Marion with many hotels and eating establishments lining the tracks near the depot. At the peak of the rail travel, approximately 50 passenger trains stopped in Marion daily. The last of which arrived on April 30, 1971. With its strong merchant-based economy, Marion provided a good way of life for its citizens. Nearby farmers brought products to market in town, using its rail system for shipping. In November of 1919, the County seat was transferred to neighboring Cedar Rapids. Trolley and bus lines made it easy for business travelers to represent their interest both in Cedar Rapids and Marion.

Marion continues to grow, not as rapid as Cedar Rapids, but certainly with as much community spirit. As industry expanded in Cedar Rapids, Marion became home to workers. Homes were built in well thought-out subdivisions. The strong pioneering spirit that has kept Marion growing is still in existence today.

Hiawatha is one of the youngest cities in Linn County. Because of its proximity to major arteries and available land, it is also one of the fastest growing areas. Hiawatha's history goes back only 50 years.

The following words are not mine, but I give to you to read:

In the 1940's, a man named Fay Clark envisioned a small town growing out of a cornfield. He bought 20 acres of land and forged a new community. He chose the site because local records showed that no tornado had ever touched down in that area. The first residents lived in mobile homes that Mr. Clark manufactured up until the Second World War when Clark switched to manufacturing military equipment. In March 1944, a fire swept through the manufacturing facility destroying everything. Mr. Clark called the Cedar Rapids Fire Department, but they refused to respond because it was outside their jurisdiction. This apparent ruin fueled his desire to build a city with its own facilities—its own fire department and its own government.

In 1950, Hiawatha was incorporated. Clark founded the fire department, the police department and the actual city. He was the city's first fire chief and police chief. He also built the city hall. It was Mr. Clark who gave the city its name, Hiawatha. Having been raised by Native American Indians, he chose the Indian name Hiawatha because he 'liked it.' Today's Hiawatha resembles nothing of the original town although Clark would likely take pleasure in seeing his vision come to life. If there isn't a 'Fay Clark Day' in Hiawatha, there should be.

This Midwestern town of Cedar Rapids has elevated itself into a place of importance here in the Heartland. The arts and culture scene is both historically and ethnically rich. According to a recent survey study, Cedar Rapids' violent crime rate is the nation's lowest among cities with populations over 100,000. Our population is around 121,000 with the entire metro area over 200,000 people. Our cost of living is approximately 8% below the national average and housing cost in the average medium range is $133,000. In Honolulu, the same average medium range is $610,000, and this price does not include a basement or a heating system.

Cedar Rapids holds a special place in my heart. Yes, it can get ugly in the winter and you want to hibernate rather than deal with the dirty snow and freezing temperatures. At the same time, you also deal with the rent, bills, and kids that are driving you crazy while being cooped up in the house. The same things people before us did while the city was being built. Maybe a person has to leave this place a while before appreciating what it has. When I die, I want to be buried in the black Iowa dirt.

When I was home recently, I drove around town looking at the old neighborhood. Our old house on the corner of 16th Avenue and 'K' Street, S.W. is still there, green siding and all. The two pine trees are gone. The house at 20th Avenue and 'L' Street is completely gone because of Interstate 380 passing through that area, along with much of the old neighborhood. The hill in Linwood Cemetery is still there, but it seems smaller and the area is now neatly maintained. The surrounding woods have also disappeared.

Deborah Drive, out off Wilson Avenue has become a shady, tree-lined street. A quiet, pleasant street just like before, and there lies ahead, Jones Park, in all its glory. The swimming pool looked much like it did back in 1960. The young saplings in the park are now huge and beautiful. There's no pond, however, but still a lot of room with acres of neatly mown grass that seems to go on forever. I didn't get down to Prairie Creek and the train trestle but I'm sure the creek is still rolling along towards the Cedar. Mothers in the area, still shouting after their kids. "Stay away from the water, if you know what's good for you!" Nostalgia swept over me as I slowly drove the long way back to my mom's house with a smile on my face.

THE END

'A person who publishes a book appears willfully in public with his pants down.'
Edna St. Vincent Millay
October 2004 Writer's Digest

Copyright Infringement and Plagiarism Disclaimer

I did extensive taking of the entire structure and topical sequence of original copy and used complete passages verbatim.

I never claimed those words I used as my own and placed disclaimers before each chapter before copying the information I found from the work of others.

I also placed the names of all individuals and organizations I used or gained information from in the Acknowledgement section of this book.

Steve Childs 2004

ABOUT THE AUTHOR

The author was born at St. Lukes Hospital in Cedar Rapids, Iowa. He was raised in Cedar Rapids and graduated high school at Jefferson Sr. High School where he became a two time Iowa state wrestling champion.

He wrote this book for his mother and family to reminisce with. Then realized it could become something for the citizens of Cedar Rapids to enjoy reading. And also, for the former, current and future students of Jefferson High in Cedar Rapids, Iowa.

Mr. Childs lives in Honolulu, Hawaii.